EMPIRICAL MODELING AND ITS APPLICATIONS

Edited by **Mamun Habib**

Empirical Modeling and Its Applications
http://dx.doi.org/10.5772/61406
Edited by Mamun Habib

Contributors

Seonghoon Jeon, Chaoyu Yang, António Carrizo Moreira, Victor Moutinho, Jorge Mota, Olga Maltseva, Kleomenis Kalogeropoulos, Christos N. Chalkias, Nikos Stathopoulos, Efthimios Karymbalis, Roberto Sarmiento, Raul Ignacio Hernandez, Cesar Mendez-Barrios

Published by InTech

Janeza Trdine 9, 51000 Rijeka, Croatia

Publishing Process Manager Edi Lipovic

Technical Editor SPi Global

Cover InTech Design team

First published July, 2016

Printed in Croatia

Additional hard copies can be obtained from orders@intechopen.com

Empirical Modeling and Its Applications, Edited by Mamun Habib

p. cm.

Print ISBN 978-953-51-2493-1
Online ISBN 978-953-51-2494-8

For EU product safety concerns:
IN TECH d.o.o., Prolaz Marije Krucifikse Kozulić 3, 51000 Rijeka, Croatia,
info@intechopen.com or visit our website at intechopen.com.

Meet the editor

Dr. Md. Mamun Habib is an Associate Professor at Asia Graduate School of Business (AGSB), UNITAR International University, Malaysia. Prior to that, he was involved with the Department of Operations Research/ Decision Sciences at Universiti Utara Malaysia (UUM), Malaysia. He is the Editor-in-Chief of International Journal of Supply Chain Management (IJSCM), London, UK (SCOPUS Indexed). He has 15 years of experience in the field of teaching for graduate and postgraduate students, as well as in training, consultancy, research and Ph.D. supervision. As a researcher, Dr. Habib published 75+ research papers, including conference proceedings, journal articles and book chapters/books. Also, he serves as the Editor-in-Chief/Lead Guest Editor/Editor/Editorial Board Member/Reviewer of more than 20 journals, particularly Scopus and ISI Indexed Journals. He delivers lectures as keynote speaker at various international conferences.

Contents

Preface

To my beloved father who lies at Jannatul Baqi (Madinah, Saudi Arab), Late ***Alhaj Md. Habibur Rahman (69)***, for his lifelong enormous inspiration to achieve excellence.

Empirical modeling has been a useful approach for the analysis of different problems across numerous areas/fields of knowledge. As it is known, this type of modeling is particularly helpful when parametric models, due to various reasons, cannot be constructed. Based on different methodologies and approaches, empirical modeling allows the analyst to obtain an initial understanding of the relationships that exist among the different variables that belong to a particular system or process. In some cases, the results from empirical models can be used in order to make decisions about those variables, with the intent of resolving a given problem.

In the first Chapter, empirical models of the total electron content are presented through comparative study. Majority of them provide an adequate accuracy and reliability. As the basic application of TEC measurements the problem of determination of maximum concentration NmF2 of the ionosphere with use of its equivalent slab thickness τ is considered. It is remarkable that existing models of τ are not global and do not provide sufficient accuracy in determining NmF2. Therefore, an approach for new global model is demonstrated in this chapter.

Chapter 2 highlights a model that can be used to improve the accuracy of seagrass mapping, to simulate the propagation of light. The researchers explored that the appropriate wavebands for seagrass mapping generally lie between 500 to 630 nm and 680 to 710 nm as well. The chapter provides an improved algorithm to retrieve bottom reflectance and map the bottom types that would be meaningful for management and preservation of coastal marine resources.

Chapter 3 describes the application of empirical modeling to the estimation of shipping costs in a Mexican manufacturing firm. The findings depicts that overall transportation costs using an empirical model tend to be lower than costs calculated by a previous model. This demonstrates the practical and potential utility that results based on empirical modeling can have in a real-life setting.

Chapter 4 illustrates the extended history of GIS modeling and to converse the modern observes in terms of integration of GIS with the hydrological modeling. Water resources management and catchment analysis are crucial aspects of the twenty-first century in hydrological and environmental sciences. Thus, hazard assessment and risk evaluation modeling have become a strategic aim and an extremely useful tool for stakeholders, decision makers and scientific community.

Chapter 5 introduces the actual applications of critical loss analyses in these cases, and remarks on several issues brought in the course of applications. The SSNIP test is a well-known conceptual framework of market definition for competition policies in most countries. Critical loss analysis is a practical method that implements the principle of SSNIP test in a quantitative way to determine whether the relevant market for an antitrust case should be enlarged or not.

There is an important gap in the literature on the promotion of competition in electricity markets in what pertains to the analysis of two different streams: the absence and presence of regulation. Accordingly, chapter 6 analyzes the interactions among market power indexes, marginal costs and bidding strategies in the two mentioned scenarios, for comparative purposes. Although there is some literature on this issue, the main novelty of this chapter is the discussion of the regulatory implications that could have been adopted in order to control and mitigate the market power, to encourage new investments in new technologies and to recover sunk costs with the transition to a competitive market.

The book entitled "Empirical Modeling and Its Applications" encompasses six (6)chapters. From that point of view, the concept of the book solely depends on the contributors of the book chapters. Therefore, special thanks and gratitude must go to the book chapters' authors. However, review process is also very lengthy but significant in order to ensure uniqueness of the book chapters. The jobs of reviewers are highly appreciable. In addition, the Editor acknowledges a great debt to InTech Publisher for publishing this book on time.

On the eve of this publication, the Editor wishes to acknowledge and thank his beloved mother, *Alhaja Shirin Habib*; his spouse, *Dr. Farzana Afzal*; his two kids, *Rafiul Habib* and *Farzeen Habib*; and other family members for their tireless encouragement to complete this book.

Last but not least, I express gratitude to the Almighty for spiritual inspiration and guidance in the completion of this publication.

Assoc. Prof. Dr. Md. Mamun Habib
Asia Graduate School of Business (AGSB),
UNITAR International University,
Malaysia

Chapter 1

Empirical Modeling of the Total Electron Content of the Ionosphere

Olga Maltseva and Natalia Mozhaeva

Additional information is available at the end of the chapter

http://dx.doi.org/10.5772/62837

Abstract

With the appearance of such satellite systems as GPS, GLONASS, Galileo, and others, the total electron content TEC measured by means of navigational satellites became a key parameter characterizing a state of the ionized space. In turn, functioning of navigational and telecommunication systems needs models of TEC for an estimation of accuracy of positioning, for the short-term and long-term prediction of this parameter. In this Chapter, empirical models of the total electron content are presented. The new result is their comparison. It is shown that the majority of them provide an adequate accuracy and reliability. As the basic application of TEC measurements, the problem of determination of maximum concentration NmF2 of the ionosphere with use of its equivalent slab thickness τ is considered. It is shown that existing models of τ are not global and do not provide sufficient accuracy in determining NmF2. An approach for new global model is offered.

Keywords: empirical modeling, ionosphere, total electron content, positioning, equivalent slab thickness, disturbances

1. Introduction

All processes on the Earth are related to the influence of the sun. Under the influence of solar radiation, the Earth is surrounded by an ionized shell, which is called the ionosphere. The role of the ionosphere in ensuring mankind activity cannot be overestimated: It softens the blow of the solar wind and provides wave propagation of various frequency ranges. The simplest example is the variety of communications systems that are affected by the ionosphere and are described in detail in [1]. Among them may be selected satellite communications, satellite navigation, including systems such as GPS, GLONASS, Galileo and others, space-based radars and imaging, terrestrial radar surveillance and tracing, and others. For the operation of navigation and communication systems, the most important parameter is the ionospheric total electron content TEC modeling capabilities and the use of which is the subject of this Chapter. TEC parameter is defined as the number of electrons in the atmospheric column of 1 m^2 and is measured in units of TECU, where TECU = 10^{16} electrons/m^2. Methods for measuring the TEC are described in detail in [2]. Due to the complexity and diversity of the ionospheric processes, different approaches to the modeling of ionospheric parameters were developed. Empirical (or statistical) models based on statistical analysis of the results of measurements in different parts of the globe for a long period of time are widely used. Empirical models describe some mean states of the ionosphere, so they cannot be used to describe, for example, ionospheric disturbances. However, such models are widely used because they are easy and convenient way to describe and predict the behavior of the ionospheric parameters. Considering the disturbed conditions is possible by adaptation of models to parameters of current diagnostics. The big need for such models leads to the development of various new options. In this Chapter, two methods of modeling the TEC will be considered: (1) the integration of theoretical or empirical N(h)-profile (Section 2) and (2) empirical models (Section 3). It will focus on assessing the proximity of new models to the experimental data. The presence of well-known advantages of monitoring TEC (a large number of receivers, continuous global monitoring, and data availability on the internet) has made TEC appealing to determine NmF2 (same foF2). To do this, we need to know the proportionality factor—the equivalent slab thickness of the ionosphere τ. Section 4 is devoted to simulation methods of τ.

2. Methods based on the integration of N(h)-profiles

Such methods are considered by the example of the most widely used model of the International Reference Ionosphere (IRI), which developed from the late 60s [3] under the auspices of Committee on Space Research (COSPAR) and International Union of Radio Research (URSI). Model IRI constantly modified, in particular, to improve the definition of the TEC, it has been modified three times in this century: in 2001, 2007, and 2012 [4–6], however, a satisfactory compliance with the experimental values failed, as illustrated by several examples. This paper uses a new version of the IRI-IRI-Plas [7], which includes elements not found in previous versions: (1) a new scale height of the topside ionosphere, (2) expansion of the IRI model to the plasmasphere, (3) adapting the model to measured value of the TEC. Section 2.1 includes a brief description of the model. Any new model should be tested on experimental data, so in Section 2.2, the results of testing this model according to the incoherent radar sounding, data of satellites CHAMP and DMSP, tomographic reconstructions are presented. In Section 2.3, the TEC values for new and previous versions of IRI are compared to experimental values and conditions in which modeling results are the best specified.

2.1. Description of IRI and IRI-Plas models

At present, the IRI model is the international standard for determining ionospheric parameters [8]. This is the statistical average model based on the huge amount of data of ground and satellite measurements. For the problems of wave propagation, its most important parameters are as follows: critical frequency foF2 of the F2 layer (or the maximum concentration NmF2, a linear relation with the square of the critical frequency), maximum height hmF2, propagation coefficient M3000F2 determining the maximum usable frequency MUF for the path length of 3000 km, altitude profile of the electron density N(h), the total electron content. Defining the parameters is made using coefficients CCIR and URSI, obtained by Fourier expansion according to the "1960s," 1980s. Start parameters are the indices of solar activity. The input parameters are the date, latitude, and longitude of points on the globe. The adaptation of the model to the current diagnostic parameters (foF2, hmF2) and correction of disturbed conditions using the storm-factor SF [9] are provided. There are several basic versions of the model reflecting the most important stages of its modification: IRI79, IRI90, IRI95, IRI2001, IRI2007, IRI2012 [3–6]. The 2007 modification has two options [5]: IRI2007corr and IRI2007NeQ. The first option is a correction factor for the model IRI2001. The second option is a model of the topside ionosphere NeQuick [10]. At present, there is a new version IRI-Plas [7], which can be considered as a new modification of the model IRI, although in fact, it exists more than 12 years [11]. The main distinguishing features of this model are as follows: (1) the introduction of a new scale for the height of the topside ionosphere, (2) expansion of the IRI model to the plasmasphere, (3) ingestion of experimental values of TEC.

2.2. Testing the model IRI-Plas according to various experiments

Since one of the reasons for the discrepancies of measured and model TEC is the shape of the profile, this section presents the results of testing the model IRI-Plas according incoherent sounding radar ISR and satellites CHAMP and DMSP. Data of ISR is very seldom. We managed to gather them for the some stations on the globe. Results have been obtained for European stations StSantin, Tromso, Svaldbard, and for the American station Millstone Hill, Japanese Shigaraki, station Arecibo in Puerto Rico, from [12]. **Figure 1** shows the results for the station StSantin. The first panel includes the N(h)-profile of the initial model, that is, profile, calculated by the model values of foF2 and hmF2. It is represented by symbol IRI (black circles). The symbol foF2 (squares) indicates N(h)-profile obtained by adapting the model to the experimental values only foF2. Triangle (symbol TEC) shows the profile obtained by adapting the model to the experimental values only TEC. The crosses show the profile for the model, adapted to the experimental values of the two parameters foF2(obs) and TEC(JPL). The hollow circles show the values measured by radar. One valuable source of information is the measurement of plasma frequency on satellites, flying at various altitudes. In the second panel, N(h)-profiles are compared with plasma frequency of satellite CHAMP (h ~ 400 km), in the third panel—with DMSP (h ~ 840 km).

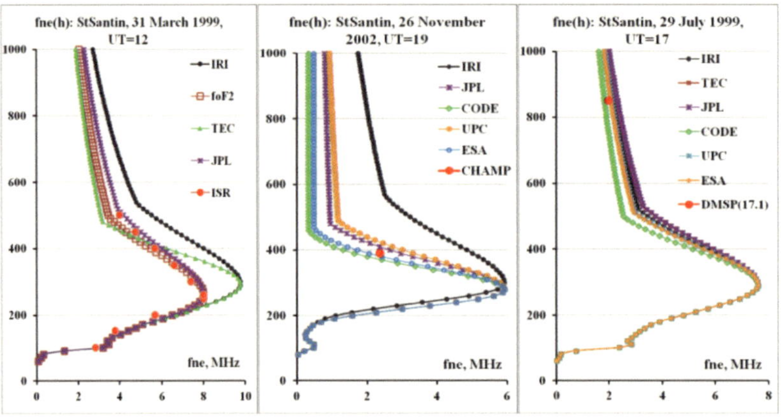

Figure 1. Comparison of model and experimental N(h)-profiles above the station StSantin.

The initial IRI model and its adaptation to only the TEC do not always provide a match with the profile of ISR. Coincidence is achieved only when adapting models to both parameters TEC and foF2. Similar results were obtained for the remaining stations. Reference [13] presents N(h)-profiles of Kharkov radar for conditions of low solar activity. The results for the two profiles of this series are presented in [14]. Increasing the statistics show that there may be differences, but in most cases this applies to the bottomside profile, which does not give a large contribution to TEC. Thus, despite the limited amount of data, we can conclude that the adapted profiles are quite close to the radar and satellite data at various points of the globe. The results for satellites CHAMP and DMSP are compared for the original IRI model and the model adapted to an experimental values foF2 together with TEC of one of the global maps (JPL, CODE, UPC, ESA). Square shows the plasma frequency. In cases where the flight time does not coincide with the time of TEC observation, this is indicated in parentheses. All the results show that the model and the experimental critical frequency can vary greatly, but the most important result is that through the point with the plasma frequency can pass multiple profiles, that is, measurement on separate low-flying satellites do not provide unambiguous profile. Unambiguity can be provided by use of data of simultaneous flights of two satellites [15].

2.3. Comparison of model and experimental values of the TEC

Methods for determination of the TEC have both similarities and differences. These differences lead to the differences of the TEC values for different methods. Reference [16] gives an example of the differences in the specific days on 25 and 28 April 2001 for the station Kiruna. Below in **Figure 2**, the TEC values are given for these days and other stations in various parts of the globe, as well as a comparison with the model values for the medians, because the models provide the medians. In the graphs representing the results for specific days, black circles show the values of the map JPL, squares—TEC of the map CODE, triangles correspond to the map UPC, crosses—the map ESA. In addition, asterisks show values for medians of the model

IRI2001, circles and pluses present values of two options of model IRI2007 (corr and NeQuick), rhombs—values of the model IRI-Plas.

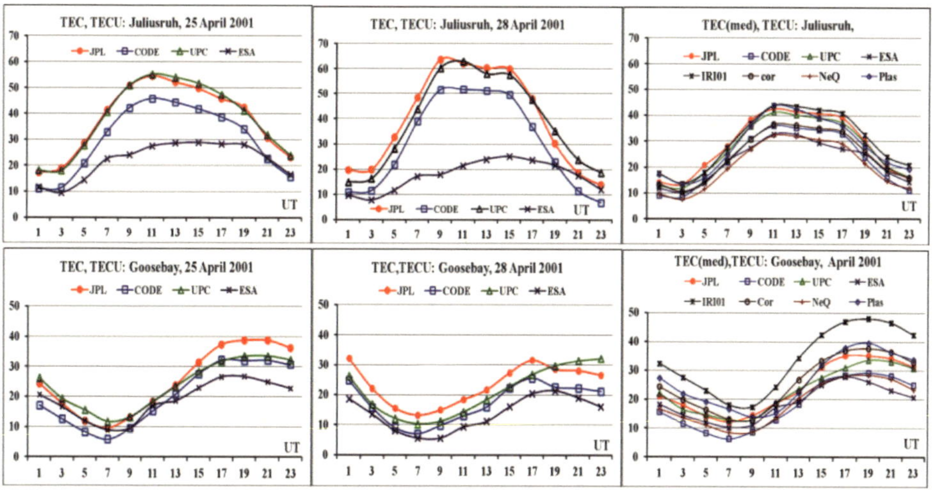

Figure 2. Comparison of TEC according to the stations Juliusruh and Goosebay.

Significant differences may be seen from day to day, for example, of two days, the maximum value may be either for the map JPL (in most cases), and maps ESA or UPC. Quantitative assessment of conformity of experimental and model values can be illustrated with the help of absolute and relative standard deviation (SD) for the monthly median, considering the value of the map JPL as a reference. The results are given in **Tables 1** and **2** for stations Juliusruh (54.6°N, 13.4°E), Moscow (55.5°N, 37.3°E), Manzhouli (49.4°N, 117.5°E), Goosebay (53.3°N, 60.4°W), Thule (77.5°N, 69.2°W), Ascension Island (7.9°S, 14.4°W), Grahamstown (33.3°S, 26.5°E), Port Stanley (51.7°S, 57.8°W). In the **Table 1**, the absolute standard deviation is given, in **Table 2**—the relative standard deviations.

JPL	CODE	UPC	ESA	IRI01	cor	NeQ	Plas
Julius	6	1.67	7.56	3	4.76	8.39	2.64
Moscow	4.69	3.02	7.17	2.16	3.66	6.64	2.60
Manzh	6.27	5.37	4.97	4.31	7.41	7.45	5.60
Goose	5.85	1.86	6.19	10.05	2.20	5.55	3.52
Thule	9.22	3.36	7.82	11.07	2.13	11.50	5.67
AscIs	3.81	8.02	8.67	10.57	12.82	12.61	21.04
Grah	6.11	3.50	8.35	4.52	4.45	4.19	5.26
PortS	3.41	6.50	7.02	10.09	6.81	7.60	9.34

Table 1. Absolute RMS deviations of the different values of TEC from TEC (JPL), TECU.

JPL	CODE	UPC	ESA	IRI01	cor	NeQ	Plas
Julius	20	5.80	26.33	9	16.57	29.24	9.20
Moscow	15.68	10.09	23.97	7.23	12.23	22.21	8.68
Manzh	17.22	14.73	13.64	11.82	20.34	20.44	15.38
Goose	24.35	7.74	25.77	41.84	9.16	23.10	14.66
Thule	36.95	13.47	31.32	44.36	8.54	46.07	22.72
AscIs	1.93	7.78	9.03	10.09	13.36	13.08	17.93
Grah	19.00	10.88	25.96	14.05	13.83	13.04	16.36
PortS	12.98	24.71	26.70	38.37	25.88	28.89	35.49

Table 2. The relative standard deviations from the values of TEC(JPL), %.

RMS differences for different maps when compared with the map JPL in a large range of latitudes and longitudes do not exceed 10 TECU, and the smallest differences were obtained between JPL and UPC. It makes 5–35%. Comparison of absolute deviations for different models shows that the best fit with the map JPL was provided by version "corr" of the IRI2007 model, for which the standard deviation does not exceed 10 TECU. The IRI-Plas model gives better results than IRI2001, except the equatorial station Ascension Island.

Thus, with a few exceptions model can provide values of TEC differences not exceeding the difference between the maps.

3. Methods of the empirical modeling

The empirical modeling of TEC, to which Section 3 is devoted, plays a huge role both for the prediction of TEC, and for testing models of type described in Section 2. For modeling TEC, basically, the method of orthogonal components [17, 18] is used; however, authors do not submit corresponding coefficients and functions. In Section 3.1, the simplest model of Klobuchara [19] is brief stated as it was unique for updating of delay of signals in an ionosphere many long years and till now is widely used for systems with single-frequency receivers though the authors using her have identified several weaknesses, for example [20]. Section 3.2 describes model [21] as an example of a model for a particular station, which should have a high degree of accuracy. The model is based on the values of biases given by the Laboratory JPL. This paper presents the results of an additional test showing that there are difficulties and for this type of models. Section 3.3 describes a new model NGM **(the Neustrelitz Global Model) [22], which in addition to the TEC model includes models of other parameters (NmF2, hmF2) [23, 24]. The authors of this model have conducted their own testing, but for definite conclusions about the effectiveness of the model, it is not enough, so the results of more extensive testing will be presented in Section 3.3. Section 3.4 describes the latest models of the TEC [25].

3.1. The model of Klobuchar

The model of Klobuchar was developed in the mid-seventies and includes one layer with infinitesimal thickness at height of 350 km. Slant TEC is calculated in a cross-point of a ray with this height. The model provides a delay estimation (in sec) for a day and night ionosphere along a vertical direction, using eight coefficients transmitted in the navigational message. The night correction is supposed to equal constant DC, fair on a global scale, in five nanoseconds (~1.5 m). The day delay is defined in the form of a cosine $T^V_{iono} = DC + A\cos[2\pi(t - \Phi)/P]$ where A is amplitude, P is period, Φ is a phase depending on the geomagnetic latitude of under ionospheric point, T^V_{iono} is a vertical delay. Eight transmission coefficients of two polynomials of 3° include four coefficients for A and four coefficients for P. Controlling ground segment of GPS updates these coefficients according to the season and the level of solar activity. Phase Φ in the argument of the cosine is constant and equal to 14 h. If the argument $[2\pi(t - \Phi)/P]$ is greater than $\pi/2$, the cosine becomes negative, and T^V_{iono} includes only a constant DC. Delay along the line is calculated as $T_{iono} = F * T^V_{iono}$ where $F = 1 + 16(0.53 - El)^3$, El—the angle of elevation. Taylor expansion of the equation for T^V_{iono} gives an expression for the model of Klobuchar.

This model serves as a standard when comparing the effectiveness of the correction of the ionospheric delay.

3.2. Taiwan empirical model of TEC

The majority of empirical TEC models of new generation are statistical. In reference [21], some models were built for a single point (24°N, 120°E) using the biases of JPL laboratory from 1998 to 2007 for quiet geomagnetic conditions (Dst > −30 nT). Input parameters are local time (LT), day of the year (DOY), the index of solar activity (F10.7 or EUV). Since the choice of the best index from their huge number is not obvious, the authors [21] investigated the effect of this choice on the final result. Set of indexes included the average values of F10.7 and EUV for the period from 1 to 162 days. It most closely matches the model and experimental values of the daily TEC caused EUV, which provided standard deviation RMS = 9.2TECU compared with 15-day moving medians with their RMS = 10.4TECU and evaluation for IRI2007 version NeQuick RMS = 14.7TECU. Daily values of index EUV (0.1–50 nm), obtained by Solar Heliospheric Observatory SOHO, were taken on a site http://www.ngdc.noaa.gov/stp/SOLAR/ftpsolarradio.html. The functions have periods of variations in 6, 8, 12, and 24 h with a dominant period of 24 h. Synodic period, causing variations in solar index about 27 days, was clearly identified in the spectrum of the TEC variation, as well as semiyear variations of 183 days, year (332 days), and longer (609 days). TEC is the product of three functions of three parameters (EUV, DOY, and LT). The function describing the dependence on solar activity uses a cubic approximation. The factor of the seasonal dependence includes three harmonic multipliers, daily course includes four harmonics. DOY parameter is normalized by the number of days in a year. The coefficients αn are presented in [21]. It should be noted that these coefficients are given in truncated form in the article, and this can lead to errors. Examples of correspondence between model and experimental values are given in **Figure 3** (calculations were performed using the full set of factors, kindly provided by one of the authors [21]). The results for August 2002 presented in [21] and our calculations coincide. This makes it possible to obtain the results for other months of 2002 and for the same months of low activity.

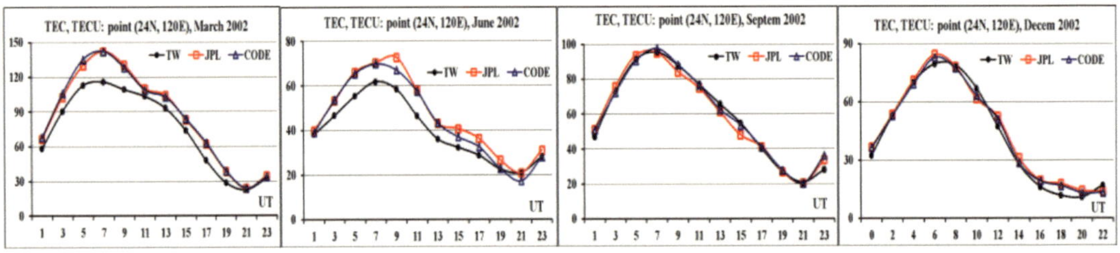

Figure 3. Comparison of model and experimental TEC for the Taiwan model near the peak of solar activity.

It is perfectly visible seasonal variations of TEC at the given latitude and full compliance for autumn and winter months. In the spring and in the summer, the model underestimates values. RMS range is 4–14 TECU. The relative standard deviation amounts to 6–18%. For a minimum of solar activity, TEC values were 2–3 times less than at the maximum of solar activity. The model can both underestimate and overestimate the experimental values. The range of the absolute deviation was 1–10 TECU. If we compare these results with a 50% rating for Klobuchar model [19], we get improvement in 2–5 times. Traditionally, the comparison is made for the medians, because the model is median, and the definition of instantaneous values is not possible. But the model [21] provides instantaneous values. **Figure 4** gives a comparison of the daily model and experimental values for August 2002.

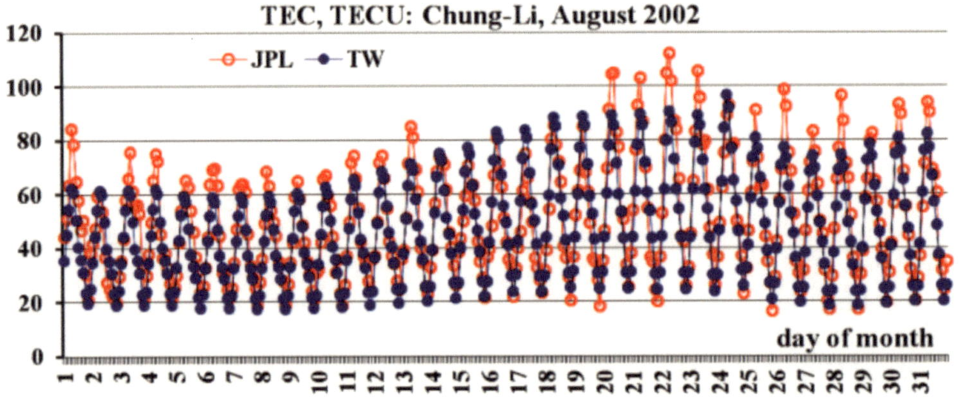

Figure 4. Comparison of daily model and experimental values of TEC for August 2002.

Good correspondence of dynamics of TEC variations that are confirmed by quantitative estimations of absolute deviations 6.4 TECU is visible. RMS of absolute deviations is 8.3 TECU, and relative deviations are 16.4%.

These results show high efficiency of the model and a way of its construction. It can be used for testing of other models.

3.3. Empirical model NGM

The NGM unlike the Taiwan model is global. Its structure can be described as follows. Model TEC (NGM) is given by product of five multipliers: TEC = Ф1 * Ф2 * Ф3 * Ф4 * Ф5 [22]. Each multiplier reflects dependence on the certain physical factor and is calculated with use from two to six coefficients. Coefficients are defined by a method of least squares superposition on experimental data for some years. Multiplier Ф1 describes dependence on local time LT, that is, on an zenit angle of the Sun, and includes daily, semidiurnal, 8-day variations. It is calculated with use of five coefficients. Multiplier Ф2 describes annual and semi-annual variations, using two factors. Multiplier Ф3 includes dependence of TEC on a geomagnetic latitude. The model includes equatorial anomaly in latitudinal course of TEC. Dependence on the solar activity is described by index F10.7. The model for NmF2 [23] includes 13 factors. The maxima of a daily course of TEC and NmF2 are fixed at LT = 14. The model for hmF2 [24] includes four factors. Data-ins are: doy—number of day in a year, D(21.3)—number of day on 21 March in a year (80 for not leap, 81—for leap), F10.7—monthly average value of index F10.7 for the concrete day, ϕ—a geographical latitude of a point, λ—a geographical longitude of a point, ϕm—a geomagnetic latitude of a point, sign $\sigma = \phi/|\phi|$, LT(array)—an array of local times. TEC in various latitudinal zones strongly differ on the properties; therefore, results are presented separately for each zone. Comparisons for a middle-latitude zone are illustrated on an example of European station Juliusruh. As all models are median, comparison is performed for monthly medians. Typical examples are given in **Figure 5** for the conditions close to a maxima (2001) and minimum (2007) of solar activities. The first drawing shows absolute deviations |ΔTEC(med)| for 2001. In this case, comparison is carried out for two versions of the IRI model: IRI2001 and IRI-Plas to estimate, whether can improve model IRI-Plas results of the previous versions. The second drawing gives relative deviations σ(TEC(med)). Next drawings concern to 2007.

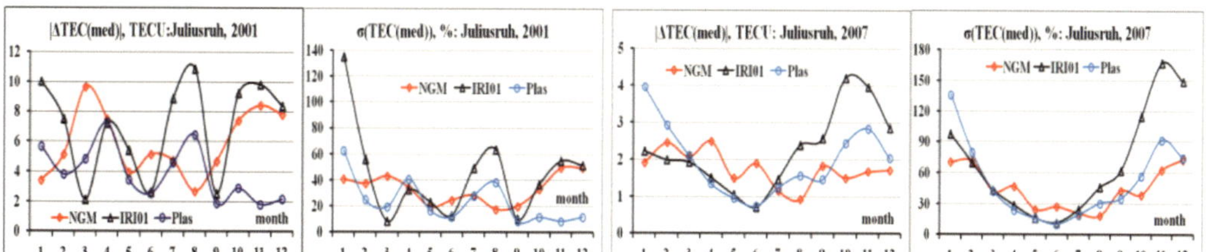

Figure 5. Examples of comparison of results in the conditions of a maxima (2001) and a minimum (2007) of solar activities for middle-latitude station.

There are months when the NGM model provides the better results than both IRI models; however, in winter months, all models do not provide necessary correspondence with experimental data. The particular interest is represented by results for high and equatorial zones. In some papers, for example [26], the possibility of use of the IRI model in high latitudes was shown. If in middle latitudes, the results of comparison can be similar for several stations, in high latitudes due to a strong variability it is possible to expect differences; therefore, results in **Figure 6** are given for several stations with various coordinates. It has appeared that results for high-latitude stations not strongly differ from results of middle-latitude station with some increase of deviations with a latitude.

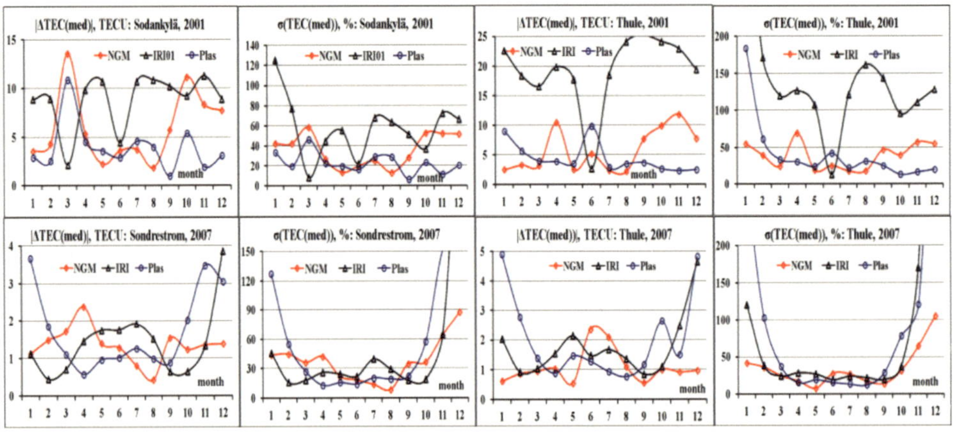

Figure 6. Comparison of daily courses of foF2 and TEC medians for high-latitude stations in the conditions of low (2007) and high (2001) solar activities.

Maximum deviations concern to the IRI2001 model, illustrating advantages of models NGM and IRI-Plas before this model. At comparison of results for models IRI-Plas and NGM, advantage has the IRI-Plas model. In the conditions of low solar activity for all stations, there are periods when deviations for the NGM model are less than for the IRI model. Absolute deviations are lower in maxima of solar activity, and relative deviations are higher. The big deviations are inherent in all models in winter months. For a low-latitude zone, results are illustrated on an example of the data of station Athens (**Figure 7**), for equatorial—Ascension Island (**Figure 8**).

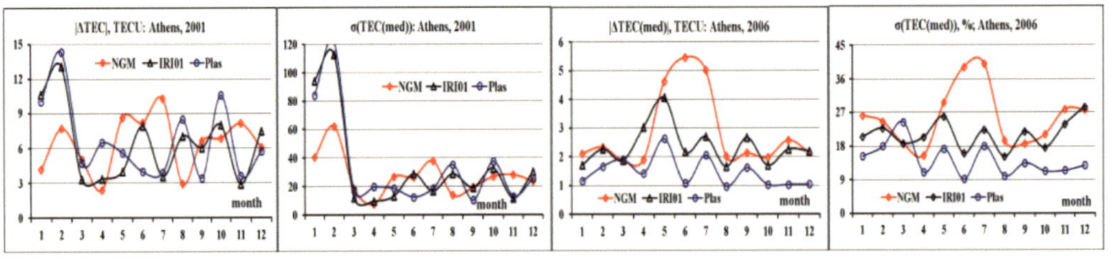

Figure 7. Comparison of annual dependences of TEC medians for various models in 2001 and 2006 for station Athens.

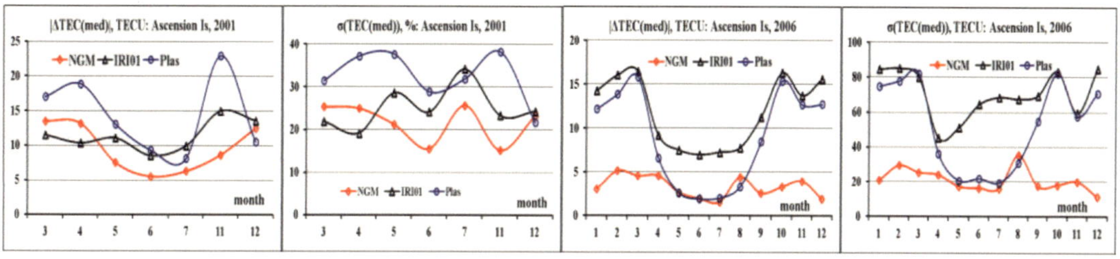

Figure 8. Comparison of annual dependences of TEC medians for various models in 2001 and 2006 for station Ascension Island.

For low-latitude station Athens, the NGM model has not advantages before remaining models, but for the equatorial station Ascension Island, the big advantages are visible; however, it is not obvious that the same results will be for other equatorial stations. More detailed results are presented in [27]. Results for separate stations yet do not give an overall picture. It is interesting to reveal behavior of deviations depending on a latitude. Results are given in **Figure 9**. They concern to certain month and a longitudinal zone: European (April 2002 and July 2004) and American (April 2002 and November 2003). Cases were selected on the basis of the greatest number of stations.

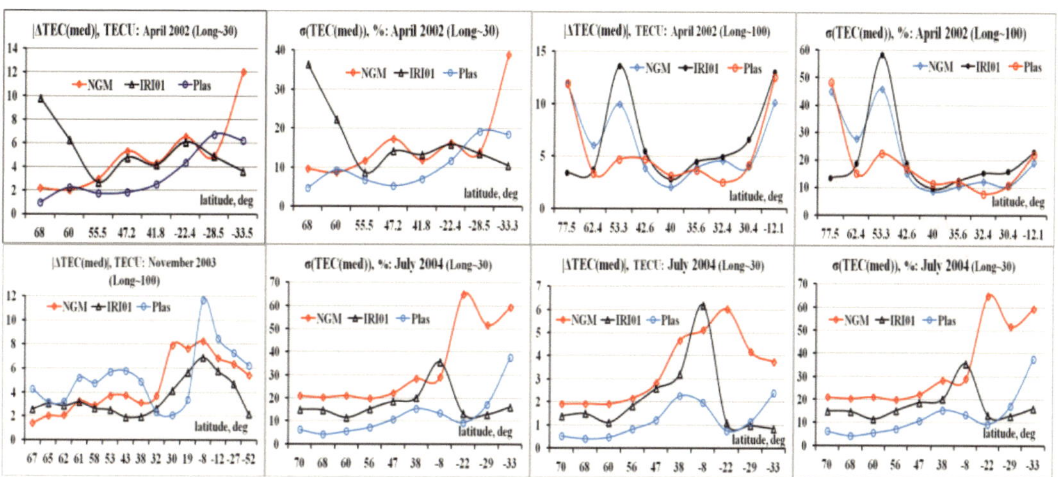

Figure 9. Examples of latitudinal dependences of medians for various conditions.

Graph shows ranges of latitudes in which this or that model has advantages; however, for other conditions results can be others. The best results in most cases concern to the IRI-Plas model. It is important that in most cases relative deviations do not exceed 20%. This is comprehensible result.

3.4. The Bulgarian global empirical model of TEC

Process of a model development goes continuously. This is an additional confirmation of an urgency of this process. The model [25, 28], on the one hand, is most physically justified, on the other hand, by estimations of authors of [25], their model is two times more exact, than the NGM model. In references [25, 28], it was developed not only the TEC model, but also the model of its error [28]. Difference from the NGM model is the taking into consideration not only the components caused by sunlight, but also regular wave structure of the tidal nature acting from the lower atmosphere. The model is constructed according to the map CODE for 1999–2011. Sliding medians are calculated by means of a 31-day window, and the median is assigned to central day of a window, that is, 16 numbers. Sliding medians are calculated independently for each point of the chosen grid. Daily data sets for each modified geomagnetic latitude, a geographical longitude, and time UT are obtained. One of the reasons of use of the modified geomagnetic latitude instead of geographical just also is the account of influence of the lower atmosphere and a thermosphere as this influence depends on a configuration of force lines of a magnetic field. The difference between geomagnetic and geographical frames generates an additional tidal response of the ionosphere. Spatial-temporary structure of TEC is represented in the form of [29]: TEC = Φ1 * Φ2 * Φ3. Function Φ1 is represented in the form of expansions in Taylor series, Φ2 and Φ3—in Fourier series. As parameter of solar activity, it is chosen not only index F10.7, but also its linear velocity KF. The seasonal factor includes 4 harmonics: the annual, semi-annual, 4 and 3 monthly. The daily variability includes three components: mean value TEC, a part describing solar components, and a part describing stationary planetary waves. The model includes 4374 constants which are defined by a method of least squares. The number of included components in Taylor's and Fourier's expansions is defined by a trial and error method with use of the following criterion: Components of higher order are rejected if their inclusion improves an error only in the third sign. In papers [25, 28], detailed investigation of deviations of model TEC values from observational ones by means of estimations of an average (regular) error (ME), a mean squared error (RMSE), standard deviation errors (STDE) was conducted. For all array of the used data, the following estimations are obtained: ME = 0.003TECU. For such value of ME, the other values are RMSE = STDE = 3.387TECU. These estimations are compared to estimations for the NGM model of TEC [22]: ME = −0.3TECU, RMSE = 7.5TECU. Thus, the Bulgarian model has a smaller error in two times. However, it is noticed that both models are climatological, that is, describe an average condition in quiet geomagnetic conditions, and the difference in number of coefficients (12 against 4374) is underlined. Authors [25] absolutely fairly do not consider a higher number of coefficients as a model shortage as these factors are calculated once; however, they are unavailable. Coefficients of the NGM model were published and can be used by any user. In turn, we can notice that in an error distribution of any model there are "tails" and it is important to define, which latitudinal zones and which conditions of solar activity they concern to. As any model cannot work equally well in all latitudinal zones and meet the possible requirements because of limitations of the approaches, the used data, distinction of physical processes, testing of models does not cease to be an actual problem.

In conclusion of this section, we will note reference [30] in which some methods were compared at an estimation of positioning accuracy. One of them is based on the TWIN model [31]. This model was used in [32] for correction of ionospheric delays in single-frequency receivers and has yielded results of positioning accuracy better than the Klobuchar model and standard global maps of TEC. Figures lay within 1–10 m. These figures and other results of the reference [32] show that basic distinctions between accuracies of positioning for these models are not present, but the TWIM model is constructed by data for low solar activity. The example for high activity is given in the paper [30] mentioned in [32]. In it, results of six methods were compared: (1) not corrected delays, (2) model [19], (3) IRI2001, (4) the prediction for 40 min by results of tomographic reconstructions, (5) a method of tomographic reconstructions MIDAS, (6) a two-frequency delay (it was used as a true delay). The basic emphasis was made on an estimation of a possibility to use a tomographic method for increase of positioning accuracy. As advantages, it is indicated a possibility of an obtaining of the data in real time though it demands presence of an infrastructure which does not exist yet in many regions. In methods 4–5, tomographic maps of N(h)-profiles were used for delay calculation. Results were obtained for the European zone and four stations: MAR6, GOPE, VILL, ANKR for several days of year 2002, and period 21 October–4 November 2003. By results of paper [30], it is possible to make **Table 3** in which results are given in order of accuracy increase.

	Non-comp		Klobuchar		IRI2001		Forecast		MIDAS	
	Mean	**Max**	**Mean**	**Max**	**Mean**	**Max**	**Mean**	**Max**	**Mean**	**Max**
MAR6	10	18	4	10	3	6	1.5	3	0.5	1.5
GOPE	11	20	3	9	3	6	1.5	3	0.5	1.5
VILL, ANKR	13	20	4	9	3	6	1.5	3	0.5	1.5

Table 3. The positioning accuracy provided by various methods, by results of [31], in m.

Feature of reference [30] is the estimation of the positioning accuracy during the strongest geomagnetic perturbations which have paralyzed work of many satellite systems [33], however in [30] optimistic enough results are obtained at use of method MIDAS though conclusions have ambiguous character.

4. Use of a median of the equivalent slab thickness of the ionosphere τ for determination of NmF2

The presence of known advantages of TEC measurement (a great number of stations, continuous global monitoring) has made TEC attractive to calculation of NmF2 (the same foF2) in a global scale. For this purpose, it is necessary to know a constant of proportionality—an equivalent slab thickness τ of the ionosphere. Values of τ(IRI) are most often used [20, 34]. The surprising fact: There is a considerable quantity of publications in which morphological features of τ(obs) are described, but nobody has guessed to use it for calculation of NmF2.

Probably, it was because practically nobody compared τ(IRI) and a median τ(med) of observational τ(obs). In Section 4.1, comparison of two types of τ is carried out and deviations of the calculated foF2 values from experimental magnitudes foF2(obs) are obtained. In Section 4.2, effectiveness coefficients Keff of use of a median τ(med) in comparison with τ(IRI) have introduced. Values of Keff will be presented as for separate stations of globe, and on a global scale, and it is shown that these coefficients for τ(med) are always higher than 1 unlike coefficients for τ(IRI). To use τ(med) on a global scale, it is necessary to have its model. The mention of a possibility of construction of the τ model practically does not meet in papers. Some variants are possible: (1) construction of superficial function of kriging using values of τ(med) in several points, (2) two-parameter model on the basis of hyperbolic approximation τ(hyp) = b0 + b1/NmF2, (3) the NGM model, (4) the IRI-Plas model. The doubts are stated in the paper [35] concerning the first variant, the model of the second variant is introduced in Section 4.3. Results of testing of the third and fourth models were given in Section 3.4 and in [27].

4.1. Comparison of model and observational values of τ

Assimilation of TEC into different models became one of the directions of ionospheric modeling. Results of TEC assimilation have a direct relation to use of models in real time. Use of observational TEC(obs) together with an equivalent slab thickness τ(IRI) to calculate foF2 values can be considered as the most simple procedure of assimilation. Magnitude of τ(IRI) is calculated from a relation τ(IRI) = TEC(IRI)/NmF2(IRI) where parameters TEC(IRI) and NmF2(IRI) are medians; therefore, τ(IRI) can be considered as a median. Using of values TEC(obs) provides values NmF2(calc) = TEC(obs)/τ(IRI) and foF2(τIRI) = 8.97 *SQRT(NmF2(calc)). In reference [36], it is offered to use a median τ(med) for calculation of foF2. The following expressions are used: τ(med) = med(TEC(obs)/NmF2(obs)), NmF2(calc) = TEC(obs)/τ(med), foF2(τmed) = 8.97 * SQRT(NmF2(calc)). Thus, differences of foF2 values calculated by two ways are defined by differences between τ(IRI) and τ(med). Though there is a considerable quantity of publications in which morphological features of τ(obs) are described [37, 38], practically, there are no papers in which values of τ(IRI) and τ(med) are compared. Especially, there are no papers comparing results of use of τ(IRI) and τ(med) together with observational TEC(obs) for foF2 calculation. In the given section, such comparison is carried out. For comparison of these values, effectiveness coefficients have introduced. Effectiveness coefficients are defined by means of deviations of calculated foF2 from the observational values. |ΔIRI| = |foF2(obs) − foF2(IRI)| is a difference between instantaneous values for the IRI model and experimental values. Monthly averages were calculated. This difference stays in numerators of effectiveness coefficients. The deviation |Δτ(IRI)| = |foF2(obs) − foF2(τIRI)| defines a difference between the values calculated with use τ(IRI) and experimental foF2(obs). The deviation |Δτ(med)| = |foF2(obs) − foF2(τmed)| defines a difference between the values calculated with use τ(med), and observational foF2(obs). Coefficient KτIRI = |ΔIRI|/|Δτ(IRI)| is the effectiveness coefficient for τ(IRI). Coefficient Keff = |ΔIRI|/|Δτ(med)| is the effectiveness coefficient for τ(med). Thus, the efficiency coefficients indicate in how many times increases consistency between the calculated and experimental values in these two cases. In reference [39], differences between τ(IRI) and τ(med) are illustrated for stations in various regions of globe: Juliusruh, Goosebay, Thule, Grahamstown, Ascension Island in a daily course for July and December of several years from 2002 to 2010. In **Figure 10**, illustration of differences is given on an example of July and December for reference station Juliusruh, map JPL and moderate level of solar activity (2004).

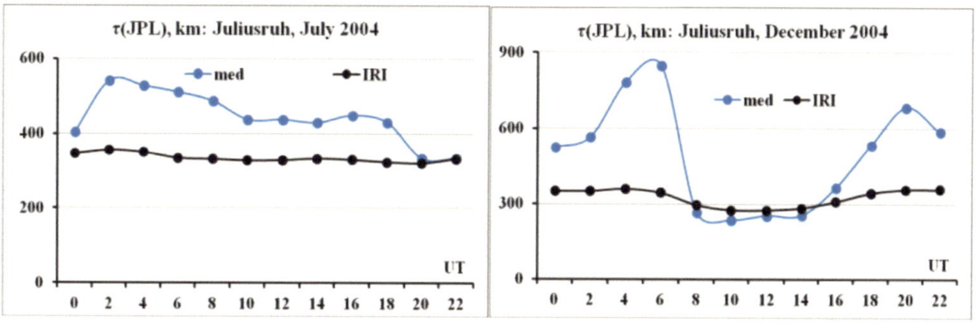

Figure 10: Illustration of differences between model and experimental values of equivalent slab thicknesses for the middle-latitude station Juliusruh of the European region.

As it is known, observational values of TEC form the whole set of maps: JPL, CODE, UPC, ESA, La Plata, IONOLab TEC, RAL, and others. The corresponding values of τ are calculated for all these values. They can strongly differ. Differences between maps can be illustrated on an example of the data of reference [40]. Considering that τ does not depend on a latitude, on graphs of work [40], all values are given in a range of latitudes and longitudes of the European zone; therefore, it is possible to see an essential scatter of values on some graphs. These graphs are of interest for us, as they concern to period of low solar activity (2007–2010) and give the chance to compare experimental τ with τ(IRI). Calculations for all 12 cases of work [40] have shown good correspondence with map JPL. **Figure 11** show results of comparison of τ(IRI) with τ(JPL) and τ (CODE) for station Juliusruh and July and December 2008. Period 2006–2009 was characterized by extremely low values of solar spots that have led to the increased errors

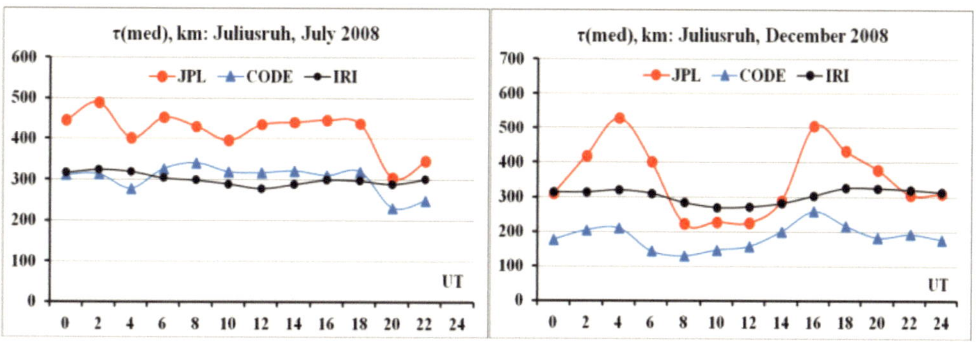

Figure 11. Comparison of behavior of monthly medians of experimental and model values τ in a daily course on an example of the European region in low solar activity.

of modeling [41]. Lack of latitudinal dependences were marked by other authors also for the European region; however, it is an essentially important point for calculation of foF2 using experimental values of TEC and medians of τ(med).

If latitudinal dependence of τ(med) did not exist, τ(med) of any ionospheric station could be used in all region for calculation of foF2, for example, by means of operative system Local Ionospheric Electron Density Reconstruction (LIEDR) which carries out monitoring of τ [35]. "Lack" of latitudinal dependence of τ is illustrated in **Figure 12** for the stations lying in a range of latitudes used in [40] for January and July 2008 for maps JPL and CODE.

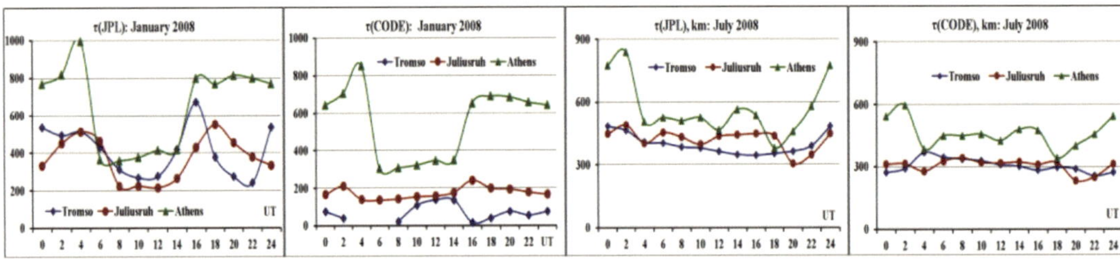

Figure 12. An illustration of differences of τ for stations with various latitudes.

It is important to investigate what deviations of foF2 leads use of this τ with such various behaviors in a daily course to. Differences between experimental foF2 values and values calculated by means of medians τ for various maps are presented in **Figure 13** for three stations of European region Tromso, Juliusruh, Athens.

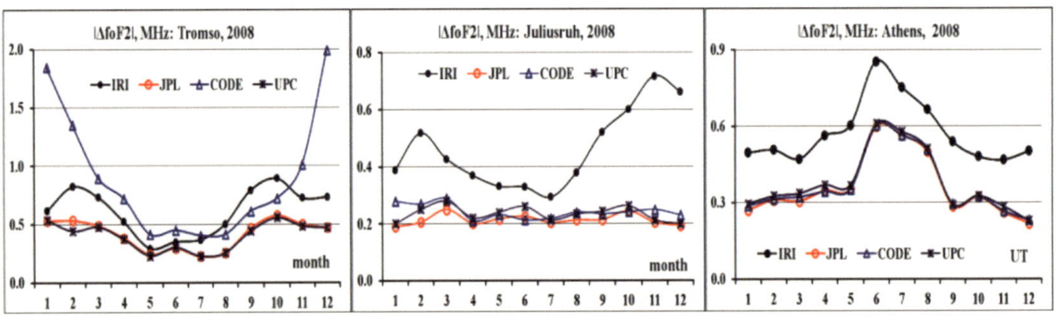

Figure 13. Deviations of calculated foF2 from experimental values for various maps.

Deviations for the IRI model are less 1 MHz. Deviations for medians of τ of global maps are 2–3 times less. It is necessary to note two important facts. For the high-latitude station Tromso, deviations for τ(CODE) exceed even deviations for the IRI model and they are maximum at night when TEC values are small. It can testify that the method of the CODE map can work insufficiently well at low TEC values. The second fact is connected rather with small differences between foF2 calculated by means of different maps and corresponding τ(med). It is a result of a good adjustment of τ(med) under TEC.

4.2. Coefficient efficiency of τ(med) usage

Since the efficiency coefficients of τ(med) are connected with the deviations, the results are given for the coefficients, and for deviations. **Figure 14** shows the deviations and coefficients of efficiency for τ(IRI) and τ(med) for the Juliusruh station. The black dots on the figures of deviations concern to the IRI model, blue circles—to the usage of traditional τ(IRI), red dots refer to the usage of the median τ(med). In all cases, the new τ provides the smallest deviation, that is, most accurately determines the critical frequency. In the right-hand parts of figures, efficiency coefficients are given for the two cases. The black line shows the points K = 1. If the ratio is equal to 1, this indicates that the usage of the equivalent slab thickness and the experimental value of the TEC provide the same results as the model itself without the involvement of the TEC. If the ratio is greater than 1, then the use of TEC gives better results than the model. If the ratio is less than 1, the use of TEC worsens results compared with the model.

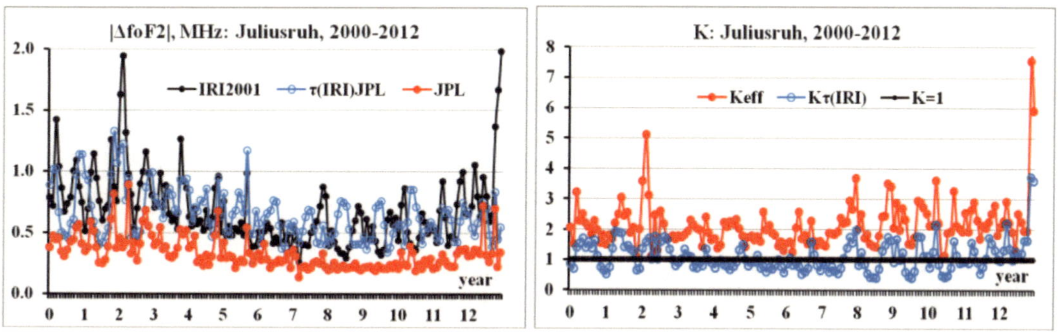

Figure 14. Deviations and coefficients of efficiency for τ(IRI) and τ(med) for the station Juliusruh.

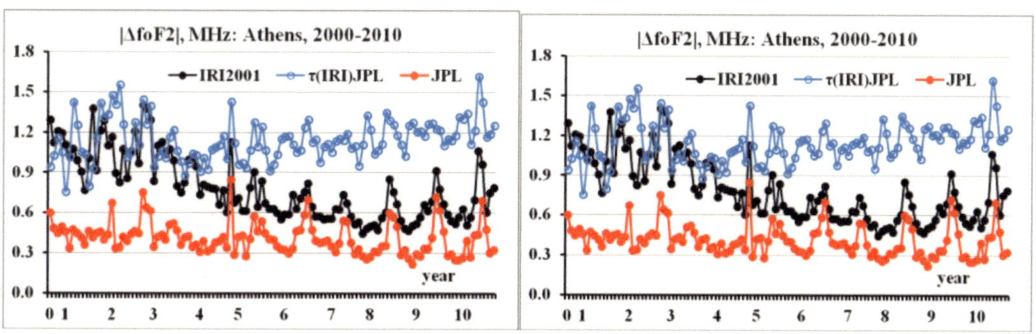

Figure 15. Deviations and coefficients of efficiency for τ(IRI) and τ(med) for the Athens.

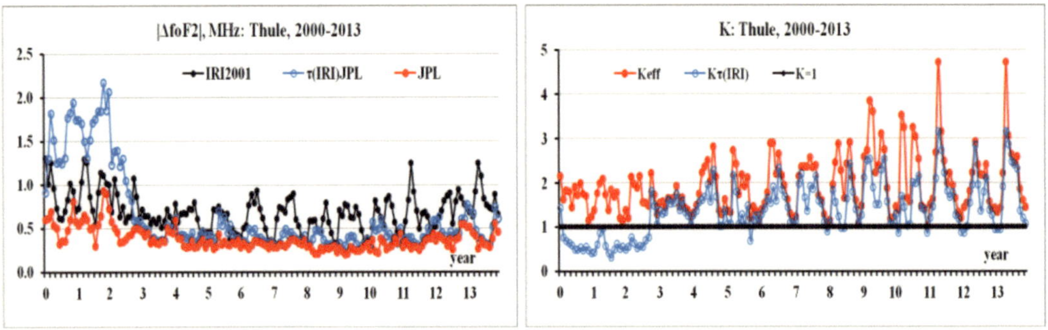

Figure 16. Deviations and coefficients of efficiency for τ(IRI) and τ(med) for the Thule.

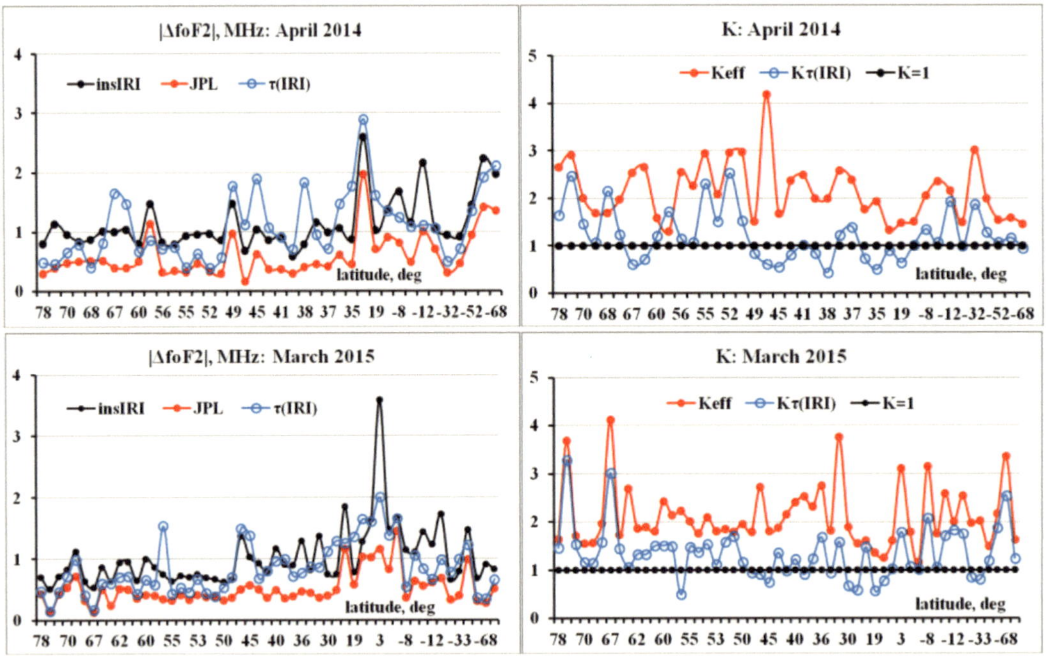

Figure 17. The global picture of deviations and efficiency coefficients for April 2014 and March 2015.

The results are shown for all months, and it would be possible to see seasonal variation, but in this case, we are not interested in such details. More importantly, that there are too many cases for τ(IRI) when the ratio is less than 1, which means that the use of TEC worsens results. For the Athens station, this situation exists almost always (**Figure 15**). It is surprising, but the best results were obtained for the Thule station (**Figure 16**). **Figure 17** give results on a global scale for April 2014 and March 2015.

These results lead to the following conclusions: (1) use of the TEC(obs) does not always improve coincidence between the calculated and experimental values of foF2 in comparison with the initial IRI model, (2) use of τ(med) leads to more exact values of foF2, (3) the coefficient Keff is always higher 1. Essential diurnal and seasonal variations are not visible. In the solar cycles including periods 2001–2011, 2002–2012, dependence of Keff on solar activity is characterized by maxima 2.5–3 in 2001–2002 and by values in a range 1.5–1.7 in remaining years.

4.3. About a global model of τ(med)

The mention of the possibility of constructing a model of τ practically does not occur in the articles, but in recent years articles on the use of TEC to determine NmF2 began to appear using equivalent thickness τ of the ionosphere. This shows the urgency of this task. In [42], the authors proposed the use of its two Neustrelitz models for the TEC and NmF2 [22, 23] to determine foF2, but without sufficient testing. These models can be named NGM (from the Neustrelitz Global Model). That is why, so much attention has been paid to comparison τ(NGM) with τ(IRI) and τ(med) in [27] and in Section 3. Authors [43] have reproached researchers that they are developing a model of the ionosphere but not a model of τ; however, authors [43] have done nothing. The latest step has been made in [44], where a model of the average values of τ was developed by using the Fourier series expansion according to the TEC and foF2 for 21 stations. Authors have taken monthly averages of the global map CODE for TEC, and monthly medians for foF2. To test the model, data from 13 stations are used in such a way to get results for multiple latitude zones (middle, low, equatorial). The results were obtained for quiet and disturbed conditions by comparison with the results of the IRI model, taking into account the STORM-factor. Formula (14) of their paper shows that the comparison is carried out not with respect to the observational values of foF2, but to this model. The assumptions made in constructing the model are as follows: (1) the linear dependence of the parameters of the TEC, foF2 and τ on the level of solar activity, (2) the lack of longitudinal dependence of these parameters at the same LT, (3) transition from a geographic to a geomagnetic coordinates does not affect the description of variations in the parameters of the ionosphere from the LT, (4) the constancy of τ in quiet and disturbed conditions. The results were obtained for the five magnetic storms of varying intensity in the period 2000–2014. They are described in detail for several stations during individual disturbances with the general conclusion that the new model provides improved compliance compared with the model IRI-STORM in middle and low latitudes and in equatorial latitudes worsens results in the quiet and in disturbed conditions. However, as shown in **Table 4** of the paper [44], the deterioration takes place in quiet conditions for the midlatitude station Chilton, and the low-latitude station Ebre. Deterioration in quiet conditions is a surprising fact, since in this case, such a model should give better results than the IRI model. As is known, the model values of TEC(IRI) are very different from the observational ones. Since the model of the authors uses the observational values of TEC, it should always lead to improvement. Consider how the behavior of τ corresponds to the assumptions of the model. The behavior of τ depending on the level of solar activity can be obtained from [39], which shows the daily variations of τ(med) and τ(IRI) for July and December in different years in the range of 2002–2010 for the stations from different latitudinal zones of the globe from auroral to equatorial (Juliusruh, Goosebay, Thule, Grahamstown, Ascension Island). This behavior includes both nonlinear changes and the constancy of the values in the daytime. Dependence of foF2 and TEC on the level of solar activity does not play a significant role since the quotient is taken. The dependences of τ(med) from RZ12 for an etalon station Juliusruh are shown in **Figure 18**.

1	2	3	4	5	6	7	8	9	10
Station	b1, b0		IRI	rec	stat	reg2	reg4	Lat1	Lat2
Juliusruh	3295.5	full	**0.73**	0.41	0.43	0.68	0.67	1.03	0.57
reg2	273.2	dist	**1.44**	0.52	0.49	0.67	0.68	1.07	0.64
Athens	5929.3	full	**0.91**	0.36	0.46	0.56	0.48	0.52	0.58
reg2	253.2	dist	**1.31**	0.44	0.74	0.52	0.59	0.87	0.51
Grahams	3788.7	full	**0.80**	0.40	0.54	0.77	0.59	0.73	0.73
Lat2	293.2	dist	**1.54**	0.46	0.62	0.84	0.75	0.82	0.77
Longyear	4947.1	full	**0.70**	0.43	0.62	0.60	0.58	0.82	0.58
Lat2	244.2	dist	**0.69**	0.49	0.73	0.69	0.69	1.01	0.63
Thule	692.7	full	**0.51**	0.14	0.15	0.56	0.42	0.47	0.59
	437.6	dist	**0.55**	0.10	0.13	0.51	0.46	0.64	0.54
Millstone	4864.4	full	**0.90**	0.50	0.47	0.48	0.46	0.67	0.49
Lat1	265.4	dist	**1.38**	0.67	0.67	0.65	0.81	0.81	0.80
Bejing	5402.8	full	**1.17**	0.49	0.61	0.61	0.58	0.70	0.62
reg4	263.9	dist	**1.99**	0.42	0.64	0.45	0.51	0.84	0.45
Kokubunji	6176.7	full	**1.29**	0.47	0.65	0.61	0.69	0.85	0.62
reg4	228.4	dist	**2.11**	0.55	0.66	0.56	0.70	0.96	0.56
Niue	4874.7	full	**1.85**	1.15	1.36	1.35	1.28	1.43	1.29
reg4	285.0	dist	**1.67**	0.71	1.00	0.73	0.85	1.11	0.67
Cocos	5467.3	full	**1.43**	0.55	0.68	0.86	0.62	0.65	0.82
Lat2	267.8	dist	**1.66**	0.52	0.77	0.88	0.67	0.80	0.83
Mawson	1466.2	full	**0.91**	0.27	0.37	1.00	0.85	1.02	0.92
Lat2	386.8	dist	**1.12**	0.12	0.21	0.80	0.98	0.98	0.81

Table 4. Deviations of frequencies, calculated by hyperbolic dependence, from the experimental values of March 2015.

For July, trend is visible in a linear relationship, but for transition from year to year, it cannot be. For December of moderate and low activity, there is a constancy of τ(obs) during daylight hours; in other periods, linearity is violated. With regard to the assumption 2, the authors themselves point out that the presence of longitudinal dependence may be the cause of the deterioration. Further illustration is shown in **Figure 19** for stations in various zones during March 2015, which had the largest number of stations and which also contains moderate disturbance (min Dst = −223 nT). Figures are given for τ(med) and τ(IRI) in: (a) middle latitude zone, (b) lower latitudes, (c) equatorial areas. Latitudes of stations are very close. A couple Juliusruh–Novosibirsk belongs to the middle latitudes, couples Nicosia–Kokubunji and Perth–Grahamstown, respectively, to the low latitudes of the northern and southern hemispheres. A couple Ramey–Sanya lies in the area between the low and equatorial latitudes. A couple Cocos–Darwin is closer to the equatorial zone. A couple Sao Luis–Fortaleza is in the equatorial zone. Reference [44] does not apply to high-latitude and auroral zones and, however, as in [26] the possibility of using the IRI model in these areas was shown, the results for a couple Tromso–Amderma are given.

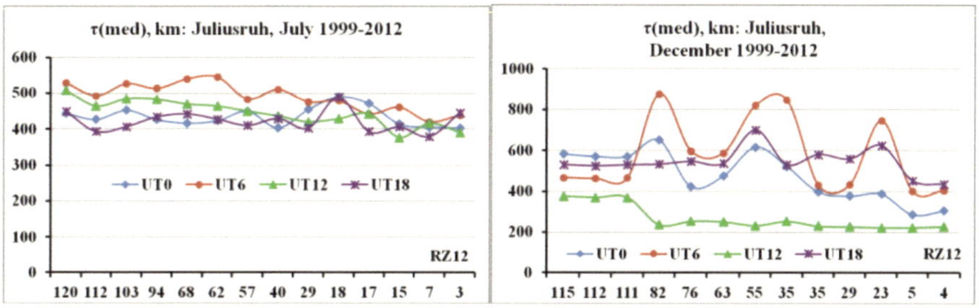

Figure 18. Illustration of τ(obs) dependence on the level of solar activity on the example of the station Juliusruh.

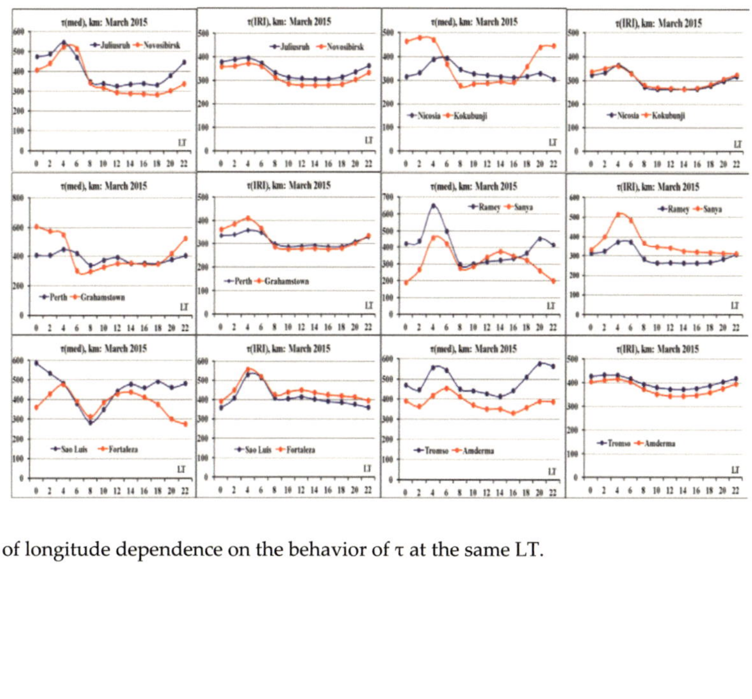

Figure 19. Effect of longitude dependence on the behavior of τ at the same LT.

We see a good agreement between the values of τ(IRI), however, large differences between τ(med). It is necessary to emphasize the differences between τ(IRI) and τ(med), which are precisely define the differences of ΔfoF2 using τ(IRI) and τ(med), reviewed in [26]. With regard to the assumption 3, if the transition is not affected, why is implemented it. Assumption 4 implies the use of the average value of τ. It goes without saying, but since the authors introduced the item, it should be noted that it is the difference between τ in quiet and disturbed conditions, especially differences from τ(IRI), are the main cause of discrepancies between the calculated and experimental values of foF2. **Figure 20** shows a comparison of τ(obs) during the disturbances with a median τ(med) and the value of the model τ(IRI) for two moderate disturbances in July 2004 with a minimum Dst = −197 nT and in December 2006 with a minimum Dst = −147 nT.

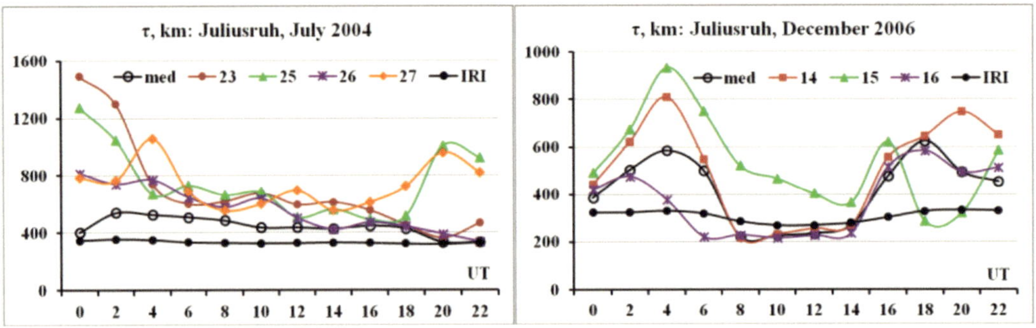

Figure 20. Illustration of differences of τ(obs) from τ(med) and τ(IRI) during the disturbances. Respective days are shown on the title of drawings.

These figures illustrate not only the difference between τ(IRI) and τ(med), but still big differences of τ(obs) from τ(med) and τ(IRI) during the disturbances. That is why, the use of τ(med) during the disturbances gives smaller deviation of foF2 than τ(IRI), but larger than the deviation in quiet conditions.

This paper also attempts to develop a global model of τ(med). In principle, there are several options: (1) the construction of a superficial function such as kriging of the values τ(med) at several points, (2) two-parameter model based on hyperbolic approximation τ(hyp) = b0 + b1/NmF2, (3) the NGM model which can be constructed on the basis of two empirical models for TEC [22] and NmF2 [23], (4) the IRI-Plas model [7, 11]. Regarding the first option in [35] were expressed some doubts. This section describes the model of the second option. Results of testing models of the third and fourth options were presented in [27] and Section 3.

Since the construction of the model using the values themselves is not possible because of the large variability of values (in particular, the pre-sunrise peak at some latitudes), we attempted to use a hyperbolic dependence on an example of March 2015 when there was the largest number of stations. For hyperbolic dependence, coefficients b0 and b1 from τ(med) = b0 + b1/NmF2 were modeled. The results are given for some of the most wide regions. The region 2 contains 8 stations of the European continent, the region 4 contains 9 stations of Far East area.

Curves for a zone of latitudes Lat1 from −52° to +65° are constructed according to 13 stations, basically, of the American continent of northern and southern hemispheres. The area for a zone of latitudes Lat2 from −68° to +78° includes 20 stations of the European, Siberian, and Southeast regions. Behavior of coefficients b0 and b1 for these regions is shown in **Figure 21**.

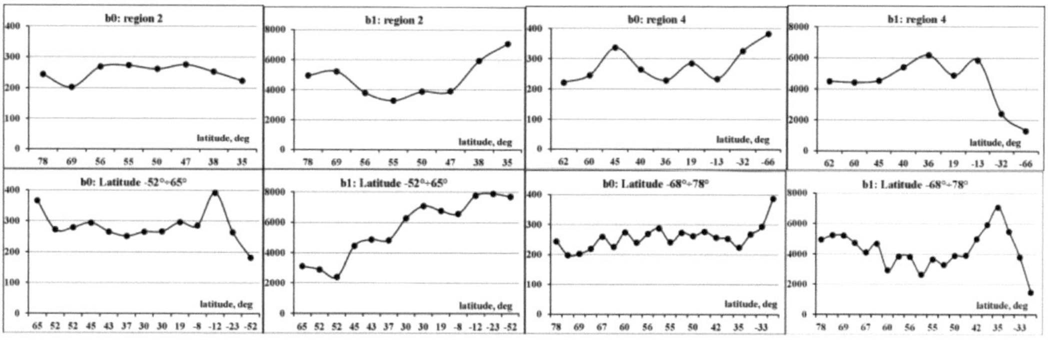

Figure 21. The behavior of the coefficients of a hyperbolic approximation for various regions.

The calculations use average values. They make up 250.62 km and 4757.36 m^{-2} for region 2, 280.21 km and 4386.01 m^{-2} for region 4, 282.92 km and 5581.81 m^{-2} for zone Lat1, 257.63 km and 4276.64 m^{-2} for zone Lat2. The results are shown in **Table 4**. This table includes the following data. Column 1 indicates the station name and the region which it belongs to. The second column shows the coefficients of the hyperbolic dependence of τ(obs) for the corresponding stations. The third column specifies the conditions which include two series of values. The top line shows average of all days of the month, at the bottom—the average for disturbed days (from 16 to 21 March). The fourth column shows the results for the initial IRI model, the fifth column—the absolute difference between the experimental values of foF2(obs) and the values calculated using τ(med) and TEC(obs). Column 6 contains the deviation of frequencies calculated using the coefficients b0 and b1 of hyperbolic approximation for a given station. Other columns give results using the coefficients of the regions indicated in the column

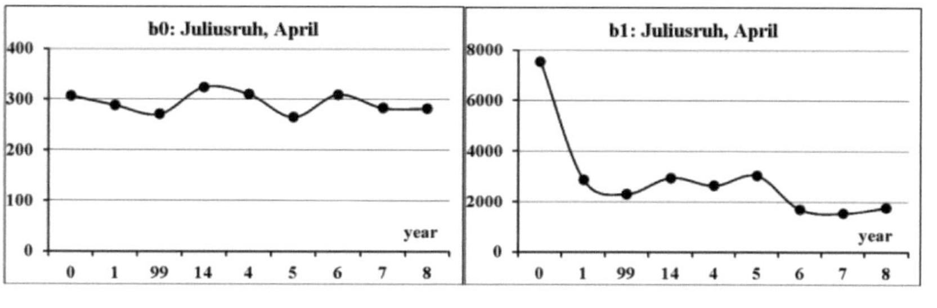

Figure 22. The behavior of the coefficients b0 and b1 of hyperbolic approximation for the Juliusruh station for April of several years.

heading. All of these values should be compared with the values for the IRI model selected in bold.

It is visible that all values are higher in disturbed days and distinctions are the greatest for initial IRI model. There is a certain possibility to use coefficients of one region for calculation of foF2 in another area. It testifies about a global character of τ(med) models. One of the important problems consists in dependence of coefficients on the level of solar activity. **Figure 22** shows coefficients b0 and b1 for the various years arranged in decreasing order of solar activity.

Another method of constructing a global model of τ(med) would be to use the coefficients $K(\tau) = \tau(obs)/\tau(IRI)$. Definite advantage of this model may be the fact that in its denominator stays the value of τ(IRI), having a global nature, and a small change in $K(\tau)$ in regions with similar longitude.

5. Conclusion

The appearance of models of the total electron content of the ionosphere TEC shows the progress made in the modeling of this parameter. This allows us to compare and use these models to forecast of TEC for any level of solar activity and to estimate the positioning accuracy. The new result is their comparison. It is shown that the majority of them provide an adequate accuracy and reliability. However, it should be noted the impact of uncertainties of their determination. These inaccuracies can be compensated using relative values, but often absolute values are needed. For four global maps JPL, CODE, UPC, ESA, solution is to construct a weighted average IGS according to four maps [45] which is also available on the same site together with the values of the maps. The main application of the TEC, discussed in this chapter, is determination of NmF2 and the critical frequency foF2 of the ionosphere. Global and continuing measurement of TEC using navigation satellites allows us to pose the problem of determining foF2 in the global scale. To do this, we need to know the proportionality factor between the TEC and NmF2, that is, the equivalent slab thickness τ of the ionosphere. It is shown that the existing models of this parameter are not global and do not provide sufficient accuracy in determining foF2. It is proposed to use the median τ(med) of the experimental values of this parameter and an approach to build its global model is presented. The advantages of using τ(med) are: (1) obtaining instantaneous values of foF2, which are especially important for the disturbed conditions, (2) calibration of TEC values for any global map or any set of experimental TEC that mitigates the impact of the uncertainty of these values.

Acknowledgements

Authors thank Southern Federal University for support (the Grant No. 213.01-11/2014-22).

Author details

Olga Maltseva* and Natalia Mozhaeva

*Address all correspondence to: mal@ip.rsu.ru

Southern Federal University, Rostov-on-Don, Russia

References

[1] Goodman JM: Operational communication systems and relationships to the ionosphere and space weather; Adv. Space Res. 2005; 36:2241–2252. doi:10.1016/jasr.2003.05.063

[2] Hoque MM, Jakowski N: Ionospheric propagation effects on GNSS signals and new correction approaches. Global Navigation Satellite Systems: Signal, Theory and Applications. Edited by Shuanggen Jin, ISBN 978-953-307-843-4, 438 pages, Publisher: InTech, Chapters published February 03, 2012 under CC BY 3.0 license. doi: 10.5772/1134

[3] Rawer K, Bilitza D, Ramakrishnan S: Goals and status of international reference ionosphere; Rev. Geophys. 1978; 16:177–181. doi:10.1029/RG016i002p00177

[4] Bilitza D: International reference ionosphere 2000; Radio Sci. 2001; 36(2):261–275. doi: 10.1029/2000RS002432

[5] Bilitza D, Reinisch BW: International reference ionosphere 2007: improvements and new parameters; Adv. Space Res. 2008; 42:599–609. doi:10.1016/j.asr.2007.07.048

[6] Bilitza D, Altadill D, Zhang Y, Mertens C, Truhlik V, Richards P, McKinnell L-A, Reinisch B: The international reference ionosphere 2012—a model of international collaboration; J. Space Weather Space Clim. 2014; 4(A07):1–12. doi:10.1051/swsc/2014004

[7] Gulyaeva TL: Storm time behaviour of topside scale height inferred from the ionosphere-plasmasphere model driven by the F2 layer peak and GPS-TEC observations; Adv. Space Res. 2011; 47:913–920. doi:10.1016/j.asr.2010.10.025

[8] Gulyaeva TL, Bilitza D: Towards ISO standard Earth ionosphere and plasmasphere model. In: Larsen RJ (Ed.), New developments in the standard model. NOVA Publishers, USA, 2011:11–64.

[9] Araujo-Pradere EA, Fuller-Rowell TJ, Codrescu MV: STORM: an empirical storm-time ionospheric correction model: 1. Model description; Radio Sci. 2002; 37(5):X1-X12. doi: 10.1029/2001RS002467

[10] Radicella SM, Leitinger R: The evolution of the DGR approach to model electron density profiles; Adv. Space Res. 2001; 27:35–40. doi:10.1016/S0273-1177(00)00138-1

[11] Gulyaeva TL: International standard model of the Earth's ionosphere and plasmasphere; Astronomical and Astrophysical Transaction. 2003; 22(4):639–643. doi: 10.1080/10556790310001722410

[12] Zhang SR, Holt SR, Zhang JM, Bilitza D. et al.: Multiple-site comparisons between models of incoherent scatter radar and IRI; Adv. Space Res. 2007; 39:910–917. doi: 10.1016/j.asr.2006.05.027

[13] Cherniak YuV, Zakharenkova IE, Dzyubanov DA: Accuracy of IRI profiles of ionospheric density and temperature derived from comparisons to Kharkov incoherent scatter radar measurements; Adv. Space Res. 2013; 51(4):639–646. doi:10.1016/j.asr.2011.12.022

[14] Maltseva O, Mozhaeva N, Vinnik E: Validation of two new empirical ionospheric models IRI-Plas and NGM describing conditions of radio wave propagation in space; Proceedings of Second International Conference on Telecommunications and Remote Sensing, Noordwijkerhout, The Netherlands, 11–12 July, 2013:109–118.

[15] Maltseva OA, Zhbankov G, Ma G, Maruyama T: Determination of the electron density in the plasmasphere using data from the GPS satellites; XXXI General Assembly and Scientific Symposium of the International Union of Radio Science August 17–23, 2014 Beijing, China (CIE). GP2. 2014:1–4.

[16] Arikan F, Erol CB, Arikan O: Regularized estimation of vertical total electron content from Global Positioning System data; J. Geophys. Res. 2003; 108(A12)1469:SIA20-1–SIA20-12. doi:10.1029/2002JA009605

[17] A E, Zhang D, Ridley AJ, Xiao Z, Hao Y: A global model: empirical orthogonal function analysis of total electron content 1999–2009 data; J. Geophys. Res. 2012; 117. A03328:1–17. doi:10.1029/2011JA017238

[18] Ivanov VB, Gefan GD, Gorbachev OA: Global empirical modeling of the total electron content of the ionosphere for satellite radio navigation systems; J. Atm. Solar-Terr. Phys. 2011; 73:1703–1708. doi:10.1016/j.jastp.2011.03.010

[19] Klobuchar JA: Ionospheric time-delay algorithm for single-frequency GPS users; IEEE Trans. Aerosp. Electron. Syst. 1987; AES-23(3):325–331. doi:10.1109/TAES.1987.310829

[20] Chen K, Gao Y: Real-time precise point positioning using single frequency data; Proceedings of IONGNSS 18th International Technical Meeting of the Satellite Division, Long Beach. CA. 2005:1514–1523.

[21] Kakinami Y, Chen CH, Liu JY, Oyama KI, Yang WH, Abe S: Empirical models of total electron content based on functional fitting over Taiwan during geomagnetic quiet condition; Ann. Geophys. 2009; 27:3321–3333. doi:10.5194/angeo-27-3321-2009

[22] Jakowski N, Hoque MM, Mayer C: A new global TEC model for estimating transionospheric radio wave propagation errors; Journal of Geodesy. 2011; 85(12):965–974. doi: 10.1007/s00190-011-0455-1

[23] Hoque MM, Jakowski N: A new global empirical NmF2 model for operational use in radio systems; Radio Sci. 2011; 46. RS6015:1–13. doi:10.1029/2011RS004807

[24] Hoque MM, Jakowski N: A new global model for the ionospheric F2 peak height for radio wave propagation; Ann. Geophys. 2012; 30:797–809. doi:10.5194/angeo-30-797-2012

[25] Mukhtarov P, Pancheva D, Andonov B, Pashova L: Global TEC maps based on GNSS data: 1. Empirical background TEC model; J. Geophys. Res. Space Phys. 2013; 118:4594–4608. doi:10.1002/jgra.50413

[26] Maltseva OA, Mozhaeva NS, Nikitenko TV: Comparison of model and experimental ionospheric parameters at high latitudes; Adv. Space Res. 2013; 51:599–609. doi:10.1016/j.asr.2012.04.009

[27] Maltseva OA, Mozhaeva NS, Nikitenko TV: Validation of the Neustrelitz Global Model according to the low latitude ionosphere; Adv. Space Res. 2014; 54:463–472. doi:10.1016/j.asr.2013.11.005

[28] Mukhtarov P, Pancheva D, Andonov B, Pashova L: Global TEC maps based on GNNS data: 2. Model evaluation; J. Geophys. Res. Space Phys. 2013; 118:4609–4617. doi: 10.1002/jgra.50412

[29] Pancheva D, Mukhtarov P, Mitchell NJ, Muller HG: Empirical model of the dynamics in the mesosphere and lower thermosphere region over the UK, including solar and geomagnetic activity; J. Atmos. Solar. Terr. Phys. 2005; 67:197–209. doi:10.1016/j.jastp.2004.07.029

[30] Allain DJ, Mitchell CN: Ionospheric delay corrections for single-frequency GPS receivers over Europe using tomographic mapping; GPS Solut. 2009; 13:141–151. doi 10.1007/s10291-008-0107-y

[31] Tsai LC, Liu CH, Hsiao TY, Huang JY: A near real-time phenomenological model of ionospheric electron density based on GPS radio occultation data; Radio Sci. 2009; 44:1–10. RS5002. doi:10.1029/2009RS004154

[32] Macalalad EP, Tsai LC, Wu J, Liu CH: Application of the TaiWan Ionospheric Model to single-frequency ionospheric delay corrections for GPS positioning; GPS Solut. 2013; 17:337–346. doi:10.1007/s10291-012-0282-8

[33] Cannon P, Extreme space weather: impacts on engineered systems and infrastructure, February 2013 Published by Royal Academy of Engineering Prince Philip House 3 Carlton House Terrace London SW1Y 5DG. This report is available online at www.raeng.org.uk/spaceweather

[34] Houminer Z, Soicher H: Improved short-term predictions of foF2 using GPS time delay measurements; Radio Sci. 1996; 31(5):1099–1108. doi:10.1029/96RS01965

[35] Stankov SM, Warnant R: Ionospheric slab thickness—analysis, modelling and monitoring; Adv. Space Res. 2009; 44:1295–1303. doi:10.1016/j.asr.2009.07.010

[36] Maltseva OA, Mozhaeva NS, Poltavsky OS, Zhbankov GA: Use of TEC global maps and the IRI model to study ionospheric response to geomagnetic disturbances; Adv. Space Res. 2012; 49:1076–1087. doi:10.1016/j.asr.2012.01.005

[37] Kouris SS, Polimeris KV, Cander LjR: Specifications of TEC variability; Adv. Space Res. 2006; 37:983–1004. doi:10.1016/j.asr.2005.01.102

[38] Jayachandran B, Krishnankutty TN, Gulyaeva TL: Climatology of ionospheric slab thickness; Ann. Geophys. 2004; 22:25–33. doi:10.5194/angeo-22-25-2004

[39] Maltseva OA, Mozhaeva NS: Obtaining Ionospheric conditions according to data of navigation satellites; Int. J. Antennas Propag. Article 804791. 2015:1–16. doi: 10.1155/2015/804791

[40] Vryonides P, Tomouzos C, Pelopida G, Haralambous H: Investigation of Ionospheric slab thickness and plasmaspheric TEC using satellite measurements. PIERS Proceedings. Moscow. Russia. August 19–23, 2012:1172–1175.

[41] Zakharenkova IE, Krankowski A, Bilitza D, Cherniak YuV, Shagimuratov II, Sieradzki R: Comparative study of foF2 measurements with IRI-2007 model predictions during extended solar minimum; Adv. Space Res. 2011; 51:620–629. doi:10.1016/j.asr.2011.11.015

[42] Gerzen N, Jakowski N, Wilken V, Hoque MM: Reconstruction of F2 layer peak electron density based on operational vertical total electron content maps; Ann. Geophys. 2013; 31:1241–1249. doi:10.5194/angeo-31-1241-2013

[43] Sardar N, Singh AK, Nagar A, Mishra SD, Vijay SK: Study of latitudinal variation of Ionospheric parameters—a detailed report; J. Ind. Geophys. Union. 2012; 16(3):113–133.

[44] Muslim B, Haralambous H, Oikonomou C, Anggarani S: Evaluation of a global model of ionospheric slab thickness for foF2 estimation during geomagnetic storm; Ann. Geophys. 2015; 58(5). A0551. doi:10.4401/ag-6721

[45] Hernandez-Pajares M, Juan JM, Orus R, Garcia-Rigo A, Feltens J, Komjathy A, Schaer SC, Krankowski A: The IGS VTEC maps: a reliable source of ionospheric information since 1998; J. Geod. 2009; 83:263–275. doi:10.1007/s00190-008-0266-1

Chapter 2

The Empirical Models to Correct Water Column Effects for Optically Shallow Water

Chaoyu Yang

Additional information is available at the end of the chapter

http://dx.doi.org/10.5772/63149

Abstract

Seagrass as one of the blue carbon sinks plays an important role in environment, and it can be tracked remotely in the optically shallow water. Usually the signals of seagrass are weak which can be confused with the water column. The chapter will offer a model to simulate the propagation of light. The model can be used to improve the accuracy of seagrass mapping. Based on the in situ data, we found that the appropriate wavebands for seagrass mapping generally lie between 500–630 nm and 680–710 nm as well. In addition, a strong relationship between the reflectance value at 715 nm and LAI was found with a correlation coefficient of 0.99. The chapter provided an improved algorithm to retrieve bottom reflectance and map the bottom types. That would be meaningful for management and preservation of coastal marine resources.

Keywords: seagrass, optical correction model, Sanya Bay, remote sensing technique, optically shallow water

1. Introduction

Given the rapid change affecting coastal environments, it is a substantial challenge to manage and preserve the coastal marine resources. It is urgent to find an effective and quantitative tool to detect such change in the optically shallow water. The spatial resolution and precision of the traditional *in situ* surveys are not enough to detect subtle changes before they become catastrophic [1, 2]. Remote sensing technique developed rapidly and can provide high spatial and temporal resolution of the benthos. Optical properties in the optically shallow waters are relatively more complex than those in the optically deep water, so the application of remote sensing technique in optically shallow waters is still in its infant stage.

An important problem with remote sensing technique in the aquatic environment is the water column effect [3, 4]. In shallow water, radiance can be affected by phytoplankton, suspended organic and inorganic matter and dissolved organic substances [5, 6].

There are several methods to correct the water column effects. The single/quasi-single scattering theory is one of them to estimate the water column contribution. Morel and Gentili [7] defined the reflectance of the optically shallow waters by removing determinations of the albedo of the substrate covering the floor. The contribution of a finite substrate to the increase in reflectance was interpreted in terms of depth if the optical properties of the optically shallow water and the reflectance at null depth of the deep ocean near the object were known. The quasi-single scattering theory [8] suggests that bottom upwelling signals can be estimated as a sum of contributions from the water column and from the bottom. A semianalytical (SA) model for mapping bottom by using the remote sensing reflectance of shallow waters was developed and most commonly cited [9, 10]. Another algorithm to compensate for water column effects is that of Lyzenga [11–13]. This model was developed from two-flow irradiance transfer. Lyzenga exploited an intrinsic correlation between two color bands. This theory was utilized to generate a pseudodepth and pseudocolor band. The pseudodepth channel can theoretically be retrieved with appropriate ground truth information to estimate absolute depth. The total remote sensing reflectance values with respect to depth were linearized by removing an optically deep water value and taking the natural logarithm of the result. Removing a deep-water reflectance value from each pixel [14, 15] or applying the water optical properties [16] which are calculated from deep waters, were used to eliminate water column influence. However, there are several issues in these methods. Because these models utilized the hypothesis that energy traveling through a water column is not related to the substrate type and water depth. In fact the intensity of light in optically shallow water decreases exponentially with increasing depth, and changes from electromagnetic radiation. The error due to the process has reduced the accuracy of seagrass mapping and bottom classification. Based on these reasons, it is necessary to consider the water depth and the diffuse attenuation coefficient when removing the water column effects.

In this chapter, we will introduce an improved optical model of incoming solar radiation transfer. This model consumed the optically shallow water as multilayer water. This effective and improved method can be applied to research the relationship between reflectance and the LAI of seagrass.

2. The improved optically shallow water model

In this algorithm the optically shallow water is considered as a plane-parallel water body and segmented into an enormous number of homogenous layers to describe the optical properties of the optically water column. In this model, it is supposed an infinitely thin layer S of thickness Δz_i at depth z existed and can be measured downward from the sensor. The ith interval covers depths from z_i to z_{i+1}, with $\Delta z_i = z_{i+1} - z_i$. Figure 1 shows that the light is incident onto the surface and scattered in all directions above the reflecting surface S. In order to calculate conveniently, we assume the reflecting surface S lies in the xy plane of a Cartesian coordinate system. In this model, z axis is vertical to the surface, S, which is described in Figure 1. The light which is incident onto the surface is defined as the incident irradiance E_d (z, λ). The subscript d represents incident and λ is the wavelength. The field of view (FOV) of the sensor and the angle of reflection are the key factors to determine if the photons scattered by the optically shallow water can be recorded by the detector (Figure 2). It is notable that attention should paid to those scattered photons which have the ability to get the sensor. We noted the unique reflected path as CO which is used to represent how the scattered photos get the sensor O. We suppose that the layer can be segmented into enormous infinitesimals. Figure 2 shows that a beam of light Φ_{di} illuminates the jth volume Δv_j of thickness Δz_i. In this situation, a fraction of the collimated incident beam is scattered by S and get into a solid angle $\Delta\Omega_j$. The spectral volume scattering function (VSF) is described as [17, 18]:

$$\beta(\psi,\lambda)= \lim_{\Delta z_i \quad 0} \lim_{\Delta\Omega_j \quad 0} \left[\frac{\Phi_{si}}{\Phi_{di}\Delta z_i \Delta\Omega_j} \right] \tag{1}$$

Where Φ_{di} is the incident flux; Φ_{si} is the scattered fraction of incident light; ψ is the scattering angle between the forward direction of the light and the line between the scattering point C and the detector O. The part of the optically water column related to the upwelling radiant flux, Φ_u^{water}, is given by [19, 20]:

$$\Phi_u^{water} = \sum_j \sum_i \beta(\psi, \lambda) \cdot \lim_{\Delta z_i \to 0} \lim_{\Delta\Omega_j \to 0} [\Phi_{di} \cdot \Delta\Omega_j \cdot \Delta z_i] \tag{2}$$

The contribution of downwelling radiant flux, Φ_{di}, is defined as:

$$\Phi_{di} = \vec{E}_d (z,\lambda) \bullet \Delta\vec{s}_j \tag{3}$$

Where $\vec{E}_d(z, \lambda)$ is the downwelling irradiance at depth z; Φ_u^{water} is the part of upwelling radiant flux and is described as:

$$\Phi_u^{water} = \vec{E}_u^{water} (z,\lambda) \bullet \vec{s} \tag{4}$$

Where $\vec{E}_u^{water}(z, \lambda)$ is the fraction of the optically water column to the upwelling irradiance.

The scattering part of the upwelling irradiance is:

$$dE_u^{water}(z,\lambda) = E_d(z,\lambda) \cdot \beta(\Psi,\lambda) d\Omega dz \tag{5}$$

Kirk [21] defined $k_u(\lambda)$ as vertical diffuse attenuation coefficient for upward flux. Then Philpot introduced the parameter in [22]. $dE_u^{water}(z \to z^-_{surf}, \lambda)$ is the part of the upwelling irradiance from the considered layer to the subsurface:

$$dE_u^{water}(z \to z^-_{surf}, \lambda) = E_d(z,\lambda) \cdot \beta(\psi,\lambda) \cdot exp(-k_u(\lambda)(z - z^-_{surf})) d\Omega dz \tag{6}$$

E_d (z, λ) can be calculated as [23]:

$$E_d(z,\lambda) = E_d(z \to z^-_{surf}, \lambda) exp(-k_d(\lambda)(z - z^-_{surf})) \tag{7}$$

Where k_d is the vertical diffuse attenuation coefficient for downwelling irradiance. $dE_u^{water}(z \to z^-_{surf}, \lambda)$ can be obtained by:

$$\begin{aligned} dE_u^{water}(z \to z^-_{surf}, \lambda) &= E_d(z \to z^-_{surf}, \lambda) \cdot \beta(\psi,\lambda) \\ &\cdot exp\left[-(k_u(\lambda) + k_d(\lambda)) \cdot (z - z_{surf})\right] d\Omega dz \end{aligned} \tag{8}$$

Equation (8) can be further simplified as:

$$\begin{aligned} dE_u^{water}(z \to z^-_{surf}, \lambda) &= E_d(z \to z^-_{surf}, \lambda) \\ &\cdot exp(-2k(\lambda)(z - z_{surf})) \cdot \beta(\psi,\lambda) d\Omega dz \end{aligned} \tag{9}$$

The total VSF $\beta(\psi, \lambda)$ can be described as [24]:

$$\beta(\psi,\lambda) = \beta_w(\psi,\lambda) + \beta_p(\psi,\lambda) \tag{10}$$

Where w and p represent pure sea water and particles, respectively. The VSF can be estimated as [25]:

$$\beta_w(\psi,\lambda)=\beta_w(90°,\lambda_0)\cdot\left(\frac{\lambda_0}{\lambda}\right)^{4.32}\cdot\left(1+0.835\cos^2\psi\right) \tag{11}$$

The particle VSF is estimated as [26]. Thus,

$$\beta_p(\psi,\lambda)=b_p(\lambda)\cdot\tilde{\beta}_p(\psi,\lambda) \tag{12}$$

Where b_p is the particle scattering coefficient and $\tilde{\beta}_p$ is the particle phase function [27–29]. Here, the Henyey-Greenstein phase function [30] is selected:

$$\tilde{\beta}_{HG}(\psi)=\frac{1}{4\pi}\cdot\frac{1-g^2}{\left(1+g^2-2gcos\psi\right)^{3/2}} \tag{13}$$

Here g is used to adjust the relative amounts of forward and backward scattering in β_{HG}:

$$2\pi\int_{-1}^{1}\tilde{\beta}_{HG}(\psi)\cos\psi d\cos\psi=g \tag{14}$$

In which case $d\Omega=sin\psi d\omega d\psi$, the contribution from the water column, can be further deduced. By substituting equations (11)–(13) into (9), the flux by the water can be estimated as (see Figure 2):

$$\begin{aligned}dE_u^{water}\left(z\to z^-_{surf},\lambda\right)&=E_d\left(z\to z^-_{surf},\lambda\right)\cdot exp\left(-2k(\lambda)\left(z-z_{surf}\right)\right)\\&\cdot\left(\beta_w(90°,\lambda_0)\cdot\left(\frac{\lambda_0}{\lambda}\right)^{4.32}\cdot\left(1+cos^2\psi\right)+\frac{b_p}{4\pi}\cdot\frac{1-g^2}{\left(1+g^2-2gcos\psi\right)^{3/2}}\right)\\&\cdot sin\psi d\psi d\omega dz\end{aligned} \tag{15}$$

The irradiance of the water can be calculated:

$$\begin{aligned}E_u^{water}\left(z\to z^-_{surf},\lambda\right)&=\int_{z_{surf}}^{H+z_{surf}}\int_{\psi_1}^{\psi_2}\int_0^{2\pi}E_d\left(z\to z^-_{surf},\lambda\right)\cdot exp\left(-2k(\lambda)\left(z-z_{surf}\right)\right)\\&\cdot\left(\beta_w(90°,\lambda_0)\cdot\left(\frac{\lambda_0}{\lambda}\right)^{4.32}\cdot\left(1+cos^2\psi\right)+\frac{b_p}{4\pi}\cdot\frac{1-g^2}{\left(1+g^2-2gcos\psi\right)^{3/2}}\right)\\&\cdot sin\psi d\psi d\omega dz\end{aligned} \tag{16}$$

Where ψ_1, and ψ_2 can be estimated as:

$$\psi_1 = -\left(\alpha_0 + \theta_0 + \frac{FOV}{2}\right) + \pi \tag{17}$$

$$\psi_2 = -\left(\alpha_0 + \theta_0 - \frac{FOV}{2}\right) + \pi \tag{18}$$

Here, FOV is the field of view of the sensor, α_0 is the solar attitude and θ_0 is the view angle measured from the z axis. Integration of equation (16), $E_u^{water}(z \to z^-_{surf}, \lambda)$ can be expressed as:

$$\begin{aligned} E_u^{water}\left(z \to z^-_{surf}, \lambda\right) &= E_d\left(z \to z^-_{surf}, \lambda\right) \cdot \left(\frac{\exp\left(-2k(\lambda)\left(z - z_{surf}\right)\right) - 1}{-2k}\right) \\ &\cdot \left[-2\pi\beta_w\left(90°, \lambda_0\right) \cdot \left(\frac{\lambda_0}{\lambda}\right)^{4.32} \cdot \left(\cos\Psi + \frac{0.835}{3}\cos^3\Psi\right)\right. \\ &\left. - \frac{b_p}{2g} \cdot \frac{1 - g^2}{\left(1 + g^2 - 2g\cos\Psi\right)^{1/2}}\right]_{\psi_1}^{\psi_2} \end{aligned} \tag{19}$$

The subsurface irradiance reflectance can be estimated [31]. $R^{water}(0^-, \lambda)$ can be further expressed as:

$$\begin{aligned} R^{water}\left(0^-, \lambda\right) &= \frac{E_u^{water}\left(z \to z^-_{surf}, \lambda\right)}{E_d\left(z \to z^-_{surf}, \lambda\right)} = \left(\frac{\exp\left(-2k(\lambda)\left(z - z_{surf}\right)\right) - 1}{-2k}\right) \\ &\cdot \left[-2\pi\beta_w\left(90°, \lambda_0\right) \cdot \left(\frac{\lambda_0}{\lambda}\right)^{4.32} \cdot \left(\cos\Psi + \frac{0.835}{3}\cos^3\Psi\right)\right. \\ &\left. - \frac{b_p}{2g} \cdot \frac{1 - g^2}{\left(1 + g^2 - 2g\cos\Psi\right)^{1/2}}\right]_{\psi_1}^{\psi_2} \end{aligned} \tag{20}$$

The subsurface remote-sensing reflectance just beneath the sea surface [32, 33], $R_{rs}(0^-, \lambda)$, can be calculated as:

$$R_{rs}\left(0^{-},\lambda\right)=\frac{R\left(0^{-},\lambda\right)}{Q} \tag{21}$$

Q is the radio of the subsurface upward irradiance to radiance conversion factor [34]. Remote-sensing reflectance of the water column just beneath the sea surface $R_{rs}^{water}(0^{-},\lambda)$ can be estimated as:

$$\begin{aligned}R_{rs}^{water}\left(0^{-},\lambda\right)=Q\cdot\frac{E_{u}^{water}\left(z\rightarrow z^{-}{}_{surf},\lambda\right)}{E_{d}\left(z\rightarrow z^{-}{}_{surf},\lambda\right)}=Q\cdot\left(\frac{\exp\left(-2k(\lambda)\left(z-z_{surf}\right)\right)-1}{-2k}\right)\\ \cdot\left[-2\pi\beta_{w}\left(90^{\circ},\lambda_{0}\right)\cdot\left(\frac{\lambda_{0}}{\lambda}\right)^{4.32}\cdot\left(\cos\Psi+\frac{0.835}{3}\cos^{3}\Psi\right)\right.\\ \left.-\frac{b_{p}}{2g}\cdot\frac{1-g^{2}}{\left(1+g^{2}-2g\cos\Psi\right)^{1/2}}\right]\Bigg|_{\Psi_{1}}^{\Psi_{2}}\end{aligned} \tag{22}$$

Finally, the bottom reflectance can be obtained by $R_{rs}{}^{b}$:

$$R_{rs}^{b}=R_{rs}\left(0^{-},\lambda\right)-R_{rs}^{water}\left(0^{-},\lambda\right) \tag{23}$$

3. Materials and methods

In situ survey was carried out in the Sanya Bay (109°25′–109°29′ E, 18°12′–18°13′ N) in the South China Sea on 15–20, April 2008(see **Figure 3**). *Thalassia* seagrass dominates in this area. Sanya Bay [35], which is a typical tropical bay, includes a broad range of habitats. Spectral irradiance was measured by using a spectrometer (S2000, Ocean Optics, Inc.) [36]. The instrument has a spectral resolution with 0.3 nm and bandwidths are from 200 to 1100 nm. Besides, a self-designed remote cosine receptor was used to measure signals proportional to the sky radiance, sea surface radiance and the radiance reflected from a horizontal reference panel by connecting to the S2000 with an optical fiber (P400-2-UV/VIS) with a FOV of 10°. The viewing angle was 40°.

Following the method in Mobley [37], the relative azimuth was set as 135°. The spectral downwelling radiance was measured from a reflectance panel $L_g(\lambda)$ (Spectralon). The reflectance of Spectralon is known, and the relationship between the measured radiance and the incident irradiance $E_d(\lambda)$ is given by:

$$E_d(\lambda)=q(\lambda)\cdot\frac{1}{\rho}\cdot L_g(\lambda) \tag{24}$$

$q(\lambda)$ is an angular and wavelength-dependent factor, and ρ_g is the irradiance reflectance of Spectralon. Clear sky conditions are necessary to in situ survey. 100 shoots of seagrass were selected to count leaf number *jj*, and also to calculate the percentage of shoots with *jj* leaves X_{jj}. Ten shoots with the same leaf number were selected. The leaves were centered on a box (25 cm×40 cm), and then took a photo to record the situation. Based on the pixels of seagrass in the photos, M_{jj}, the average leaf area of seagrass with the different numbers of leaves can be recorded. The leaf area index *M* can be estimated as:

$$M = P\times\Sigma\left(i\times M_{jj}\times X_{jj}\right) \tag{25}$$

Here *P* represents the seagrass density of each processing (shoots/m^2).

4. Results

The algorithm was employed to obtain the bottom reflectance. Based on the results the seagrass information which was retrieved from the modeled $R_{rs}{}^b$ is reasonable to. In Figure 4, between 550 nm and 750 nm the predicted value $R_{rs}{}^b$ agreed very well with the *in situ* measured bottom reflectance $R_{rs}{}^b$. Between 600 and 800 nm, $R_{rs}{}^b$ was found to be lower than subsurface remote-sensing reflectance $R_{rs}(0^-)$. This error could be related to the absorption and scattering properties of the optically shallow water which mainly affect the spectral reflectance at this band.

It is noted that the subsurface reflectance cannot be used directly to classify the bottom type or substitute the bottom reflectance. We provided a comparison between the subsurface remote sensing reflectance and the remote sensing reflectance of the bottom. The results also illustrate the conclusion in Figure 5(a). It was found that there does indeed exist a considerable difference between the subsurface remote sensing reflectance $R_{rs}(0^-)$ and the remote sensing reflectance of the bottom $R_{rs}{}^b$. Compared to the subsurface reflectance, the retrieved bottom reflectance is more related to in situ measured ones in Figure 5(b). It was found that there is a significant relationship between *in situ* measured $R_{rs}{}^b$ values and modeled ones. Therefore, it is safe to conclude that $R_{rs}(0^-)$ cannot be used directly to represent the hyperspectral recognition of seagrass in optically shallow waters is unfitted.

The seagrass reflectance with different LAI (Leaf Area Index) was surveyed to evaluate the relationship between the spectral characteristics of seagrass and also validate the sensitivity bands to LAI. The retrieved bottom reflectance can represent the typical optical properties of seagrass very well than the subsurface remote-sensing reflectance (see Figures 6(a) and (b)). Based on Figure 6(b), it is found that the typical optical characteristics of the seagrass are obvious. In addition, a spectral peak shift from the red edge to the red with leaf areas is increasing. It was found that 555, 650, 675 and 700 nm are relatively good bands to extract LAI information in Figure 6(b). In these regions, an excellent separation among the different LAI index can be done. These bands correspond to the absorption troughs and reflectance peaks, which were also related to the photosynthetic and accessory pigments. Large variations in chlorophyll contents in seagrass leaves could determine a relatively small part of leaf absorptance. Figure 6(b) shows the properties between 680 and 720 nm in the leaves' spectrum at the different sites. The evident phenomenon is related to the package effect. It was found that the pigment self-shading among thylakoid layers could affect the light absorption and the harvesting efficiency, and thereby the chlorophyll concentration is not linear with the light harvesting efficiency [38]. Cummings and Zimmerman [27], and Enriquez [28] also observed the strong package effect in seagrass, and they concluded that it attributed to the restriction of chloroplasts to the leaf epidermis. Figures 6(c) and (d) show that there is not an obvious relationship between subsurface remote sensing reflectance at 715 nm and LAI. On the contrary, there is a relatively significant relationship between the retrieved bottom reflectance at 715 nm and LAI. This phenomenon also proves that this algorithm is effective to map seagrass distribution and bottom classification.

In Figure 6(b), it was found that the reflectance of Thalassia increased from 518 to 532 nm. This phenomenon was related to the changes in xanthophyll-cycle pigmentation. In addition, the leaves of Thalassia were found to display an olive-drab color in the South China Sea, and that properties was related the peak of the retrieved bottom reflectance curve near 550 nm (see Figure 6(b)). A spectral region of maximum reflectance was found between 800 and 840 nm. It is the typical spectral reflectance of aquatic plants. Based on the spectrum analysis, the modeled bottom reflectance retrieved by the improved algorithm can be used to represent the typical optical properties of seagrass.

5. Conclusions

An improved optically shallow water algorithm was provided to model the radiation transfer. In the model, the water body was considered as a multilayer, heterogenous, nonhomogenous, natural media. The algorithm could adjust the input parameter to the equation with the different optical properties in water column for retrieving bottom reflectance. The equations which were used to retrieve bottom reflectance or to quantify the benthos can keep the same form. The method could model a wide range of the optical characteristics for radiation fields in these layers. These properties are useful to simulate any contribution of each region and learn the mechanisms of the formation of the radiation characteristics inside and outside the layers. The algorithm can appropriately minimize the effects of the optically shallow water on the remotely sensed signal to obtain an estimate of the reflectance of seagrass.

Based on the results and analysis, the method was proved to be valid for improving the accuracy of bottom mapping. The water column correction algorithm is necessary to retrieve the empirical relationships between satellite data and the interesting features in the optically shallow water. Through the implementation of the algorithm and results analysis between 500–630 nm and 680–710 nm were found to be more effective to discriminate and map seagrass meadows of the Sanya Bay. Therefore, an appropriate spectral band for seagrass mapping should include the narrow bands centered 555, 650, 675 and 700 nm (maximum bandwidth 5–10 nm). A strong correlation coefficient of 0.99 existed between the bottom reflectance at 715 nm retrieved by the water column correction algorithm and LAI. The input parameters for the algorithm in the study are the remote sensing reflectance from the subsurface. In order to apply the algorithm to the satellite images, the atmosphere correction should be taken into account. The atmosphere influence has a great contribution to affect the blue band. In order to improve the accuracy of the surface reflectance, it could be acquired through further development of the theory and models for the atmospheric correction. Therefore, the reflectance at 715 nm could be used to estimate LAI of seagrass.

Author details

Chaoyu Yang

Address all correspondence to: ycy@scsio.ac.cn

South China Sea Prediction Center, State Oceanic Administration, Guangzhou, China

References

[1] Orth, R.J. and Moore, K.A: Chesapeake bay: an unprecedented decline in submerged aquatic vegetation. Science Magazine. 1983;222:51–53.

[2] Peterson, B.J. and Fourqurean, J.W: Large-scale patterns in seagrass (Thalassia testudinum) demographics in south Florida. Limnology and Oceanography 2001;46:1077–1090.

[3] Gordon, H.R. and Morel, A: Remote assessment of ocean color for interpretation of satellite visible imagery, a review. Lecture Notes on Coastal and Estuarine Studies. 1983;4:114–114.

[4] Yang, D. and Yang, C: Detection of seagrass distribution changes from 1991 to 2006 in Xincun Bay, Hainan, with satellite remote sensing. Sensors 2009;9:830–844.

[5] Dekker, A.G., Malthus, T.J., Wijnen, M.M. and Seyhan, E: Remote sensing as a tool for assessing water quality in Loosdrecht lakes. Hydrobiologia 1992;233:137–159.

[6] Wang, C.K. and Philpot, W.D: Using airborne bathymetric lidar to detect bottom type variation in shallow waters. Remote Sensing of Environment 2007;106:123–125.

[7] Morel, A. and Gentili, B: Diffuse reflectance of oceanic waters: II Bidirectional aspects. Applied Optics. 1993;32(33):6864–6879.

[8] Smith, R. and Baker, K: Optical properties of the clearest natural waters (200–800 nm). Applied Optics 1981;20:177–184.

[9] Lee, Z.P., Carder, K.L., Mobley, C.D., Steward, R.G. and Patch, J.S: Hyperspectral remote sensing for shallow waters: 2. Deriving bottom depths and water properties by optimization. Applied Optics. 1999;38:3831–3843.

[10] Lee, Z.P., Kendall, C.L. and Robert, A.A: Deriving inherent optical properties from water color: a multiband quasi-analytical algorithm for optically deep waters. Applied Optics. 2002;41(27):5755–5772.

[11] Lyzenga, D: Passive remote sensing techniques for mapping water depth and bottom features. Applied Optics. 1978;17(3):379–383.

[12] Lyzenga, D: Remote sensing of bottom reflectance and water attenuation parameters in shallow water using aircraft and LANDSAT data. International Journal of Remote Sensing. 1981;2(1):71–82.

[13] Lyzenga, D: Shallow-water bathymetry using combined lidar and passive multispectral scanner data. International Journal of Remote Sensing. 1985;2(1):71–82.

[14] Morel, A: Optical properties of pure water and pure seawater. In: Optical Aspects of Oceanography, Jerlov, N.G. and Steemann, N.E. (Eds.): 1–24, 1974 (Academic Press, New York).

[15] Prieur, L. and Sathyendranath, S: An optical classification of coastal and oceanic waters based on the specific spectral absorption curves of phytoplankton pigments, dissolved organic matter, and particulate materials. Limnology and Oceanography 1981;26:671–689.

[16] Wayne, H.S. and Emmanuel, S.B: Calibrated near-forward volume scattering function obtained from the LISST particle sizer. Optics Express. 2006;14(8):3602–3615.

[17] He, M.X., Hu, L.B., Wang, Y.F., He, S.Y., Yang, Q., Liu, Z. and Liu, Z.S: Depth and optical properties of water column retrieved from MERIS DATA about the DONGSHA ATOLL, 2008; Available online at: http://earth.esa.int/dragon/symp2008/proceedings/10he.pdf.

[18] Gordon, H.R., Brown, O.B. and Jacobs, M.M: Computed relationship between the inherent and apparent optical properties of a flat homogeneous ocean. Applied Optics 1975;14:417–427.

[19] Gordon, H.R., Brown, O.B., Evans, R.H., Brown, J.W., Smith, R.C., Baker, K.S. and Clark, D.K: A semianalytic radiance model of ocean color. Journal of Geophysical Research. 1988;93:10909-10924.

[20] Kirk, J.T.O: The upwelling light stream in natural waters. Limnology and Oceanography 1989;34:1410–1425.

[21] Philpot, W.D: Radiative transfer in stratified waters: a single-scattering approximation for irradiance. Applied Optics 1987;26:4123–4132.

[22] Kirk, J.T.O: Light and Photosynthesis in Aquatic Ecosystems, 1994 (Cambridge University Press, Cambridge, UK).

[23] Gons, H.J: Optical teledetection of chlorophyll a in turbid inland waters. Environmental Science and Technology 1999;33:1127–1132.

[24] Conger, C.L., Hochberg, E.J., Fletcher, C.H. and Atkison, M.J: Decorrelating remote sensing color bands from bathymetry in optically shallow waters. IEEE Transactions on Geoscience and Remote Sensing. 2006;44(6):1655–1660.

[25] Becker, B.L., David, P.L. and Qi, J.G: Identifying optimal spectral bands from in situ measurements of Great Lakes coastal wetlands using second-derivative analysis. Remote Sensing of Environment. 2005;97(2):238–248.

[26] Chami, M., Mckee, D., Leymarie, E. and Khomenko, G: Influence of the angular shape of the volume-scattering function and multiple scattering on remote sensing reflectance. Applied Optics. 2006;45(36):9210–9220.

[27] Cummings, M.E. and Zimmerman, R.C: Light harvesting and the package effect in the seagrasses Thalassia testudinum Banks ex Konig and Zostera marina L: optical constraints on photoacclimation. Aquatic Botany. 2003;75:261–274.

[28] Enriquez, S: Light absorption efficiency and the package effect in the leaves of the seagrass Thalassia testudinum. Marine Ecology Progress Series 2005;289:141–150.

[29] Froidefond, J.M. and Ouillon, S: Introducing a mini-catamaran to perform reflectance measurements above and below the water surface. Optics Express. 2005;13(3):926–936.

[30] Henyey, L.C. and Greenstein, J.L: Diffuse radiation in the galaxy. The Astrophysical Journal 1941;93:70–83.

[31] Fyfe, S.K. and Dekker, A.G: Seagrass species: are they spectrally distinct? In: Proceedings of the International Geoscience and Remote Sensing, Sydney, Australia, Reising, S.V. (Ed.), 2001;6:2740–2742.

[32] Maffione, R.A. and Dana, D.R: Instruments and methods for measuring the backward-scattering coefficient of ocean waters. Applied Optics. 1997;36(24):6057–6067.

[33] Jennifer, P.C. and Kendall, L.C: Estimating chlorophyll a concentrations from remote-sensing reflectance in optically shallow waters. Remote Sensing of Environment. 2006;101(1):13–24.

[34] Louchard, E.M., Reid, R.P. and Stephens, E.C: Optical remote sensing of benthic habitats and bathymetry in coastal environments at Lee Stocking Island, Bahamas: a comparative spectral classification approach. Limnology and Oceanography. 2003;48(1, part 2):511–521.

[35] Huang, L., Tan, Y., Song, X., Huang, X., Wang, H., Zhang, S., Dong, J., Chen, R: The status of the ecological environment and a proposed protection strategy in Sanya Bay, Hainan Island, China. Marine Pollution Bulletin 2003;47:180–186.

[36] Mobley, C.D., Gentili, B., Gordon, H.R., Jin, Z.H., Kattawar, G.W., Morel, A., Reinersman, P., Stamnes, K. and Stavn, R.H: Comparison of numerical models for computing underwater light fields. Applied Optics 1994;32:7484–7504.

[37] Morel, A. and Prieur, L: Analysis of variations in ocean color. Limnology and Oceanography. 1977;22:709–722.

[38] Mobley, C.D: Estimation of the remote sensing reflectance from above-water methods. Applied Optics 1999;38:7442–7455.

Chapter 3

Least Squares Method and Empirical Modeling: A Case Study in a Mexican Manufacturing Firm

Raúl Hernández-Molinar,
Roberto Sarmiento-Rebeles and
César F. Méndez-Barrios

Additional information is available at the end of the chapter

http://dx.doi.org/10.5772/63151

Abstract

Empirical modeling (EM) has been a useful approach for the analysis of different problems across a number of areas/fields of knowledge. As is known, this type of modeling is particularly helpful when parametric models due to a number of reasons cannot be constructed. Based on different methodologies and approaches (e.g., Least Squares Method, LSM), EM allows the analyst to obtain an initial understanding of the relationships that exists among the different variables that belong to a particular system or a process.

In some cases, the results from empirical models can be used to make decisions about those variables, with the intent of resolving a given problem. The investigation describes the application of EM to the estimation of shipping costs in a Mexican manufacturing firm. The results show that overall, transportation costs using an empirical model tend to be lower than costs calculated by a previous model. This demonstrates the practical and potential utility that results based on EM can have in a real-life setting.

Keywords: empirical modeling, exploratory data analysis, least squares, linearization, transportation logistics

1. Introduction

It is well known that researchers can use empirical modeling (EM) to have a better understanding of a particular problem. This type of modeling can be improved by the expert input of analysts. When investigating a particular system or process, it is always preferable to perform both exploratory/initial and confirmatory analyses of the available data and information. Nevertheless, in some cases, it is not possible to do the latter. This means that oftentimes, professionals in positions of authority have to make decisions about important variables and problems based solely on the results from initial/exploratory models.

This chapter describes the application of EM to investigate the variables associated with shipping costs in a Mexican manufacturing firm. The objective was to obtain a model that would offer a better idea of the variables and dynamics that determine those costs. To this end, the Mexican company formed a research team tasked with a complete and detailed analysis of the problem.

Using a Least Squares Method (LSM) approach, the team proposed a new model capable of estimating transportation costs of containers shipped in vessels from Europe to a port in Mexico. Using the proposed model, the firm's management was able to make comparisons between the actual costs incurred based on a previous model (formulated by the provider of the shipping service) and the estimated costs based with the new model.

The results show that in general, cost estimates from the new model tend to be lower than those of the previous model. These results allowed the Mexican firm to start new negotiations about their shipping costs with the provider of the transportation service

2. Empirical modeling: an overview

The main objective of this section consists in reviewing the concept called EM and some other concepts employed when an investigator begins the exploration of the information. Another important objective is to suggest the use of a linear model as an important resource to clarify and propose a fitted empirical model based on the observation of the data when a special transformation process of the variables is realized.

In reference [1] comments that empirical models are guided exclusively by data. Analysts attempt to find a model that reflects trends in data to make predictions instead of explaining behavior. In particular [1] underlines the potential utility of statistical approaches/tools (e.g., regression analysis) when doing EM. As is known an empirical model can aid researchers in acquiring an initial idea of the relationship between two or more variables that are representative of a particular system or process. In spite of its inherent limitations, the results obtained using empirical models can sometimes help researchers when decisions need to be made with respect to the variables that intervene in the system/process under study.

Empirical knowledge can be understood as those instances when new information/knowledge is acquired by practical/experiential means. While this type of knowledge is undoubtedly valid and useful, it should be noted that in some cases, the conjectures/conclusions we make about observed data and results are based on the analyst's own experience and interpretation. This means that sometimes, impartiality and scientific rigor in the analysis of data and results might be difficult to achieve. Consequently, inconsistencies between the real-life problem and the

http://dx.doi.org/10.5772/63151

model proposed by the analyst can be found. It is important to consider, as reference [2] suggests, that when modeling is applied to any logistics system, flexibility must be considered.

This being said, influential thinkers and intellectuals have vigorously debated the topic of whether full certainty can be achieved with respect to the validity and representativeness of a model. For example, reference [3] argues that empirical knowledge plays an integral role in the development of so-called "scientific knowledge." This is because scientists have the opportunity to explore and confirm particular ideas/conjectures on the basis of their own empirical findings.

Under a scientific and formal context, Exploratory Data Analysis (EDA) based on empirical information requires probability and statistical concepts. However, reference [4] mentions that there exists a moment where exploratory and confirmatory data analysis must be distinguished between confirmatory nonparametric statistical data analysis, or modeling, and confirmatory parametric statistical data analysis.

It is clear that when there is no information to propose a parametric model, an exploratory analysis using empirical knowledge to obtain an initial model and solution can be justified. After this step, the analyst can judge, based on his/her expertise, whether the initial model is an adequate representation of the relationships that exists among the different variables that are part of the problem under study. Consistent with this, reference [5] also says that when it is not possible to justify the behavior of the data, an empirical model can be utilized to obtain an initial idea vis-à-vis the nature of problem of interest.

Generally speaking, EM uses nonparametric data analysis to explore trends or behaviors within the available data. It is assumed that models based on well-defined parameters and distribution functions cannot be formulated due to incomplete data/information. This type of modeling also assumes that variables belong to sample spaces where uncertainty is present.

EM can be used to represent real-life problems that require nonanalytical methods. Examples of areas/fields where EM has proven useful include industry, science, technology, engineering, medicine, biology, and management. It should also be said that more powerful computers are of immense aid when researchers use EM, especially in those situations where high uncertainty exists.

Given the uncertainty and incompleteness associated with empirical models (along with the sometimes necessary expert input of the analysts in the definition of a model), it is evident that results and information derived from these models cannot be generalized. Adding to what has been discussed already, reference [6] notes that "Exploratory data analysis seemed new to most readers or auditors, but to me it was really a somewhat more organized form—with better or unfamiliar graphical devices—of what subject-matter analysts were accustomed to do".

We now sum up some of the salient characteristics and benefits of EM: it is mainly based on observed empirical data. However, it can also include the expert judgment/opinion of analysts. The data involved in the empirical model belongs exclusively to the realm of the system or the process that is being investigated. This means that there is no input from variables, parameters, or principles that fall outside the scope of the problem under study. Empirical models are capable of generating feasible solutions that can be helpful when investigating a particular problem. This in turn can guide analysts when decisions have to be made with respect to the variables associated with the problem of interest.

In addition, two appendices are annexed to review issues about the modeling process and outline the general numerical method that uses least squares as criteria to select an empirical model.

3. Case Study: estimation of the total cost of transportation to create a future budget

3.1 Background

This section discusses the case of a firm that has operations in Mexico (heretofore referred to as MF, "Mexican firm"). We now proceed to describe briefly the problem at hand: every month a sea shipment is dispatched from Europe to a port in Mexico by an affiliate of MF. Each shipment contains items that are needed for the daily operations of MF. Originally, the cost of each shipment was based on a model calculated by the company that provides the transportation service to MF. We will refer to this model as OM ("old model"). The shipping costs can vary according to the quantity of items that are being transported in the different containers included in the vessel. The combinations of items (and their respective quantities) that are transported in any shipment/container are determined according to MF's forecasted needs.

As part of their cost-saving initiatives, MF decided to investigate whether their transportation costs could be reduced. In particular, they decided to come up with their own cost-projection model to compare its estimates with those provided by OM. In this way, a more realistic estimation of their shipping costs could be obtained. To accomplish their objective, they decided to utilize historical empirical data to calculate a new model ("NM") that would provide a more accurate idea of the monthly costs associated with each shipment. Evidently, more accurate cost estimates can result in better budgeting decisions and its associated benefits.

To accomplish their objective, MF's top management made the decision to conduct a detailed analysis of the situation. A research team tasked with proposing a model that would be an adequate representation of the problem was formed. One of the first and most important activities of the team was the conceptualization and understanding of the different variables upon which the monthly transportation budget depends. It was observed that the cost of a given sea shipment is a function of at least one hundred variables. These variables include the value of goods, number of pallets, sea freight charges, unitary cost, and volume of the shipped items, among others.

A key step in the research process was making sure that the data pertaining to the above variables was reliable and representative of the problem to be modeled. Reference [7] warn us about the relevance in the clarification between the forecast and the planning of the variables under study. For example, MF had information about a number of variables that were not relevant to the problem (e.g., information about items that were being shipped from the USA). This meant that the database had to be depurated in great detail. Once the database was deemed reliable, the research team began to analyze the potential relationships among the set of variables of interest. Evidently, the dependent variable (transportation/shipping cost and TC) in the modeling process has to be a function of a group of independent variables such as the ones described in the previous paragraph. It needs to be specified that the main unit of analysis is the container in which the different items are transported by sea. A maritime cargo shipment usually carries several containers.

The research team examined a number of different types of models (e.g., linear, quadratic, and exponential) that could best fit the relationship between TC and its determinants [8]. After different tests and analyses, it was found that a linear model represented this relationship best. In particular, a linear model using the LSM was proposed. As is known, this method offers a best-fit model that minimizes the sum of the squares differences (errors) that exist between the real observations and the ideal results proposed by the model. The well-known general model is defined as follows:

$$\hat{Y}_i = \hat{\beta}_0 + \hat{\beta}_1 X_{1i} + \hat{\beta}_2 X_{2i} + \ \ldots + \hat{\beta}_k X_{ki} \tag{1}$$

With respect to the defining function for this problem, the research team made the decision that the final set of independent variables should be the result of all those items that appeared at least once in the historical records. In other words, if an item was recorded as being shipped and received at least once, the research team decided to include it in the general model for TC. The proposed Least Squares Model has TC as the dependent variable that is a function of potentially more than one hundred independent variables.

As will be made clear later, the quantity of independent variables to include in the model to calculate TC for a given shipment and containers will depend on previous records of shipped items. Put differently, records could suggest that TC be defined by, for example, 80 items in one month, while 70 items could be used to estimate TC in the next month.

3.2. A comparison between OM and NM estimates of shipping costs

We now proceed to exemplify the differences between the estimated costs using the model originally proposed by the transportation company (OM) and the model resulted from the analysis by MF's research team (NM). The results in **Table 1** are based on data provided by them. More specifically, the costs under the OM column reflect historical records (i.e., they are costs pertaining to completed shipments). The calculations in the NM column reflect the estimated costs had this model been used for a particular completed shipment

3.2.1. Using MLS method for estimating the total cost based on shipping part costs

It is clear that linearization process is useful when several first order variables are participating in a model reference [1]. In the present study, at least hundred variables can be interacting to define the total cost of the shipment transportation.

In this case, several variables (more than hundred) were considered to estimate the cost per shipment, for instance, value of goods, number of pallets, sea freight charges, volume, and unitary cost. After a serious selection process based on historical information and the expertise of the personal, a matrix considering shipment identifier and the cost of each of the parts is created. Using the historical information, a vector with the β_i coefficients is estimated using the LMS, and these are used to estimate the cost assigned to each shipment.

The LSM determines the best fit that minimizes the sum of squares magnitudes between the observed responses and those that are predicted by the model. A detailed explanation related to the method can be reviewed in references [9–12].

We know it is possible to predict the Y values by using the estimated model parameter values. We also know that the values can be generated from the following model

$$\hat{Y}_i = \hat{\beta}_0 + \hat{\beta}_1 X_{1i} + \hat{\beta}_2 X_{2i} + \ \dots + \hat{\beta}_k X_{ki} \tag{2}$$

The sum of the squares deviations generated from the observed values of Y and corresponding values predicted using the regression model estimated.

$$\sum_{i=1}^{n}\left(Y_i - \hat{Y}_i\right)^2 = \sum_{i=1}^{n}\left(Y_i - \left(\hat{\beta}_0 + \hat{\beta}_1 X_{1i} + \hat{\beta}_2 X_{2i} + \ \dots + \hat{\beta}_k X_{ki}\right)\right)^2 \tag{3}$$

We need to recall that least squares solution consists in finding the values of estimators

$$\beta_0, \beta_1, \dots, \beta_k, \tag{4}$$

which are called least squares estimators. The minimum sum of squares is called the residual sum of squares, the sum of squares of the error, and the sum of squares due to regression. Based on the estimated values, the estimated budget is defined for each shipment.

3.3. Constructing the estimated budget using an empirical model

Based on the linear model generated, an empirical model to forecast a budget considering the total cost on the budget is proposed. The coefficients estimates for determining the shipment cost per part in the corresponding container are generated using the Least Squares estimation method. **Table 1** shows an example for the estimation on 11 containers.

Table 2 shows the estimated values generated with the MLS method for each shipment freight. It is evident that the cost associated to the land freight is constant. The estimated cost values were determined using a multiple linear model, which consider several factors were chosen by the experienced personal in the company. The empirical model that suggests the budget for the future is showed in **Figure 3**.

Shipment freight	Container ID	OM estimates in USD	NM estimates in USD (USD)	Net difference (OM-NM)
1	1179464	2267.59	3442.27	–1174.68
2	7237802	8016.16	6661.91	1354.25
3	3311245	1871.40	1895.46	–24.06
4	9727730	7788.40	5996.43	1791.98
5	3544695	2849.20	1009.20	1839.99
6	359446	5001.89	1949.77	3052.12
7	7499748	2346.92	4122.16	–1775.25
8	1218072	5272.18	2451.45	2820.73
9	4958920	5582.10	3972.21	1609.90
10	8005021	2113.78	2570.21	–456.43
11	5503140	5578.27	4699.86	878.41
	MEAN	4310.96	3407.11	903.86
	TOTAL	48687.90	38770.94	9916.96

Table 1. A comparison between historical records of shipping costs (OM column) and estimated costs using NM for 11 containers.

Figure 1 also illustrates the calculations made in **Table 1**.

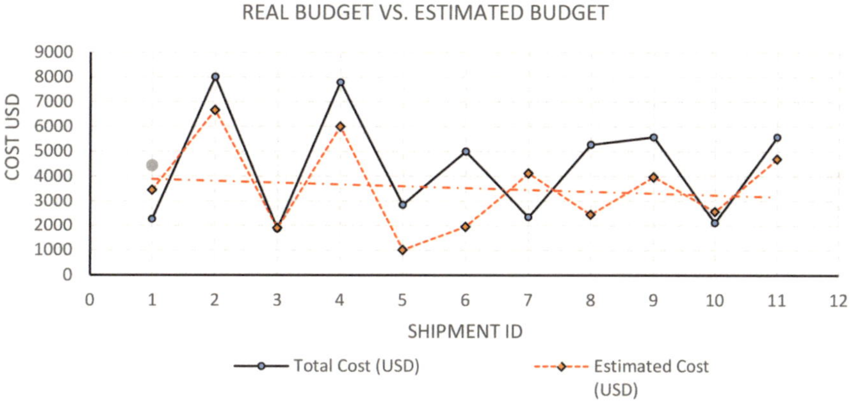

Figure 1. Real and estimated budget.

From the 11 comparisons between OM and NM estimates, it can be observed that the net difference is negative in four instances. However, the cumulative net difference shows that overall, NM offers a lower estimate of the shipping costs (savings of $9,916.96 in the total budget). This suggests that from MF's perspective, their proposed model (NM) could be used to obtain lower estimates of their transportation costs. This overall difference is made clear once the LSM estimates of both OM and NM are calculated.

Figure 2 illustrates the difference between these estimates. These two linear models have been estimated based on the OM and NM values. It is clear that NM estimates are, in general, lower than OMs. As was said before, this suggests that from MF's perspective, the use of NM's calculations would benefit them in the long run.

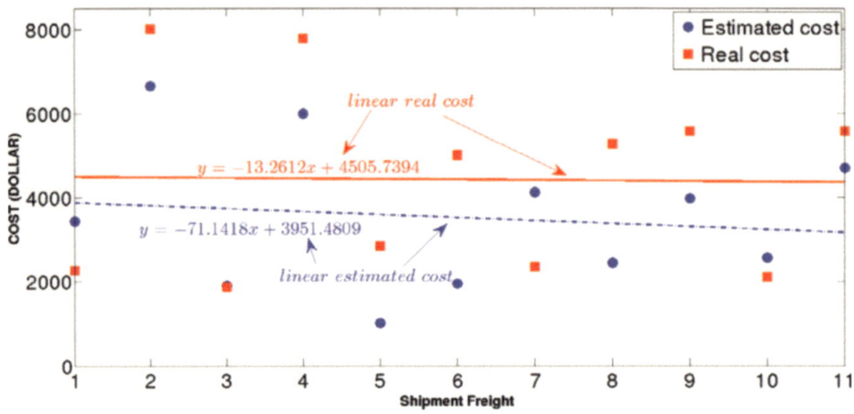

Figure 2. Comparison between real and estimated budget.

In order to probe the validity of the proposed model (NM) we can observe that in most of the cases the goodness of the model is associated with well-balanced residual values above or below a reference axis. This permits to be sure that there is no overestimation or underestimation of the predicted values.

4. Conclusion and further research

This case shows that EM can help in the forecasting process. Undoubtedly, modeling is usually a very common tool given the complexity and accuracy required in transportation problems as it is mentioned in references [2,14–19]. The described case also shows that the selection of the model is very important in any planning activity.

Despite some special programs that are able to generate the proposed models automatically, it has been made clear when information is not available or practically unknown, EM is an option that could help in the generation of structure, method, and formal knowledge. It is important to recall that the main objective in this approach is to find the best model that can represent the relationship between the variables under study, and EM is useful to do it.

The empirical model proposed is pioneering the decisions in the corporation, and it has been implemented with success. There is still interest in the improvement of criteria to upgrade the multiple linear models to estimate the containers' cost, but until now this proposal has given good results. Although this is a novel and simple approach, it is possible to mention that the combination of available data with the experience of personnel has been helpful for decision-makers.

The LSM is used as an algorithm to generate estimates for a new model that the MF has been considered sufficient and pertinent to produce significant savings. The case study has been helpful to propose the relevant data to study and estimate relations in assigning the shipping cost, based also on the experience and knowledge of the company experts. The method helped in the construction of one empirical model supported for a linearization process and has provoked significant changes in the planning process of each monthly budget.

The model proposed in this research has provided successful results, however, the team continues using other exploratory data techniques to improve it. It is expected that in the near future, it would be possible to release other options to propose better forecast of the shipment freight budget. Further studies can be conducted using parametric models generated with statistical tools or through a deep analysis using polynomials to suggest more effective transformations.

The model to forecast the shipment freight budget proposed in this research has provided successful results; this conducts to better profits and sustainable growth.

Furthermore, the research team continues using other exploratory data techniques to improve the model. It is expected that in the near future it would be possible to release other options to propose better forecasts. Also, further studies can be conducted using parametric models generated with statistical tools or through a deep analysis using polynomials to suggest more effective transformations.

Appendix A

A.1. The modeling process

A model can be conceptualized as a mathematical description which is generated using knowledge, experience, and experts opinions, but based on data that were registered previously. As references [8,13] indicate, the data help in identifying the geometric or physical tendency of a potential model and those values that correspond to characteristic values representing relevant parameters. An appropriate model suggests adjustment, or simplicity under a practical approach, and this must be conducted based on the good quality of the used information.

In general, the modeling process requires the consideration of the following issues:

- The knowledge of the system where the proposal will be applied.
- The definition of the objectives related to the activity of the system under study
- The identification of those variables that participate into the model
- A clear definition of the measurement system to quantify the variables to be revised.
- The analysis of models, algorithms, or processes that are more appropriate to get the objectives

- To achieve a detailed process of analysis of the obtained results that support the resulting alternatives
- To construct a detailed report indicating the way that the solution must be applied.

During the analysis of modelling process, the main idea is to elaborate a predictive model that helps to propose a better solution, and consequently to suggest an improvement in the indicators of the system. In order to do this is convenient for the identification of those trends or feasible models, which can be used as a reference during the process.

Another important aspect in modeling is to guarantee that data is representative of the problem under study. This requires a deep analysis of the relationships between the variables or specific sources, and to clearly point out the obtained empirical model destination.

One of the advantages in using EM is that they can conduct the right answer most of the time and does not require very formal information. This can be useful when a solution must be implemented promptly because the empirical model will be based only in the available information.

However, there is confusion about the goodness of using theoretical models instead of empirical models. It is not possible to declare that one type of model is better that the other because it depends of the specific context they are applied. The empirical models are useful when a theoretical model is not available. It is clear that the objective is to model scenarios with the best performance in order to solve a given problem or a simulation.

It is very common to apply empirical models when certain events in nature are not characterized by theoretical models, as those related to climate, air, environmental contamination, shipping, lifetime in active products, friction mechanisms trends, and etcetera.

Sometimes the use of data is not easy or is very expensive because they require long time to be obtained or not available for special causes. When this occurs, the EM is a practical option to create scenarios to simulate the behavior of the variables of interest.

It is known that many scientific, social, or engineering observations are generated through experimentation or observing the situation under study. Records of these values are stored in a data base. The information is analyzed and reported using several types of plots of the associated points.

With the available information, the investigators can apply different methods to propose formulas (equations) to formally represent the behavior of data. In most of the cases, the adjustment process considers the possibility of determining a function, to use transformed data that must be fitted to the observed values.

This approach indicates that it is very likely to propose similar results to those that a process sample would represent. Based on this, the researcher would be able to promptly represent the variables tendency under study.

A.2. Description of the modeling process

In general, the modeling process can be described in several steps. Readers interested in this topic can also review in reference [1]:

1. **Definition of problem to be solved** Most of the times this step is not formally considered. However, it is necessary to establish clearly (by written) the main objective of the generation of a modeling process. It is common that this objective changes during the searching of the solution and one must be careful in order to avoid redundancies while modeling. Normally the definition of one or more questions should be sufficient to have a reference related with the main objective. The core idea is to answer questions that are easy to comprehend.

2. **Identification and selection of the model** The investigator must select the models based on the previous knowledge or experience. It is important to consider the feasibility and the possible adjustment to data tendency. Considering that the information collected by the investigators through experimentation and observation is called empirical data, there are some scenarios that can help to understand the selection process: for example, studies that use lifetime in bearings, clinical trials, medical information, contaminant emissions, residual waters, fertilizers, or insecticides; other examples are related to costs of transportation or air conditioner failure times in flying hours of airplanes.

3. **Definition of variables** It must be considered that a variable is the observation that can have a numerical value and that this value belongs to a variable sample space. Also they are called quantiles. It is desirable that a characteristic value can be determined based on the behavior of the studied values . The idea during the modeling process is to make assumptions about the most important variable or variables in the model. This will help to detect those variables that are not useful to represent the problem under consideration. Once the variables have been identified, it is important to use specific symbols to recognize them.

4. **Calibration Model**. All models must be calibrated using available data; for instance, data can be related to lifetime on mechanisms, humans, or products. The calibration activity requires a very careful analysis making comparisons with the expected external responses. Also a thorough assessment process is required, given the importance of replication of the results in a systematic way.

5. **Validation Model**. Once the model has been calibrated, the model is validated to confirm that the behavior is well adjusted to data. Common statistical test can be achieved, for instance, the Kolmogorov–Smirnov test or a chi-squared test to guarantee a goodness of fit. Sometimes, the test is realized based on the experience or previous knowledge.

6. The validation is mandatory to review the tests that permit the verification of previously defined assumptions. Given the nature of the problem, there is no enough knowledge to describe the real analyzed system, accurately. It is necessary to take into account that all models are conceptualized based on a set of assumptions generated in the Step 1 or during the modeling process.

7. The adjusted models are used to compare against the corresponding phenomena, for example: using a well-validated model can lead in applying the property of unbiasedness. If there are other models, it is possible to analyze them at this moment. If in Steps 4 or 3, a model is not the appropriated; one can seek for other feasible models. There is the possibility that more than one model could be used, and there is an interest in propose them.

8. **Selection of the model** The valid models are chosen, and they are analyzed. Some criteria are generated to select the better option. It is possible to use the results of the tests or the comparison with other related models. It is important to consider that the models proposed can be used in the future.

9. **Implementation of the proposed model(s)** The analysis of results based on the model selected will help to simulate several scenarios useful to generate the final reports. A process of polishing is suggested in this step.

In case more or other data are collected or given the context has been changed, the iteration in the modelling process can be repeated. In general, the steps above mentioned can be summarized as is illustrated in **Figure A.1**

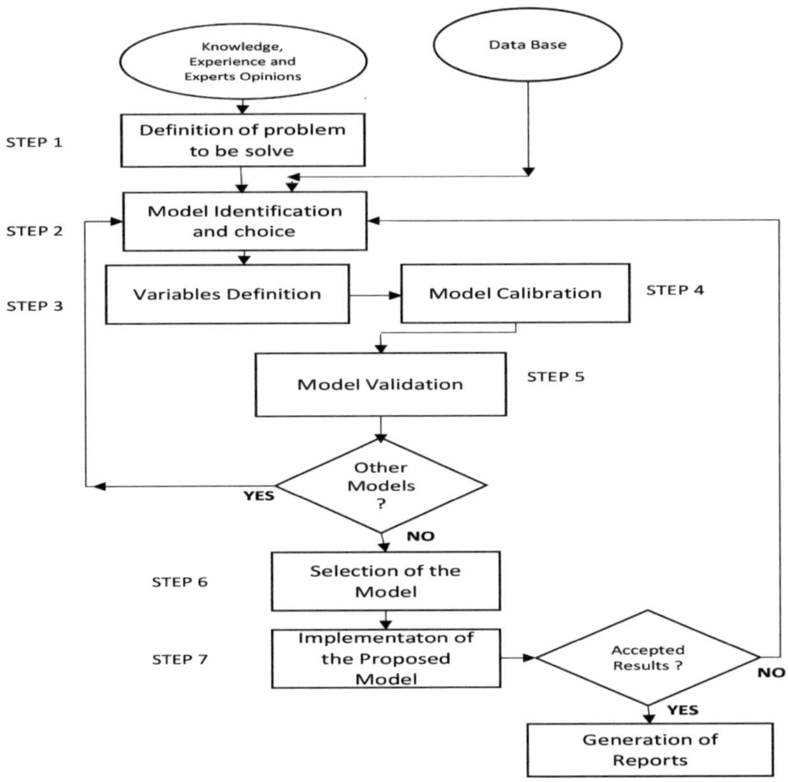

Figure A.1. The Modeling Process.

http://dx.doi.org/10.5772/63151

Appendix B

B.1. Types of empirical models

It is common to employ theoretical frameworks (based on mathematical and statistical concepts) [1,8,13] to construct models following the use of data base to define constant values. This represents characteristic values (parameters) considering a defined model.

This process sometimes is denominated the fitting model. Although the model does not adjust well to the observed data, they would be accepted; assuming the presence of some errors; and the definition is useful to explain the tendency of the studied situation. When we use this type of processes, the models are called analytical models.

In EM, it is considered that the use of data (observations) is based on sample observations or data that are coming from experiments or simple observations of the studied reality. This leads to the seeking for some trends or additional knowledge. The searching is oriented to explain the presence of certain dependent variables.

In other words, in EM, the main idea is to get rapidly the best tendency of the information and use it to find and propose a model that would be useful to make some decisions that contribute in the solution of a specific problem. **Table B.1** shows some types of typical and useful transformations to create empirical models.

Type of model	Function	Mean features
Linear	$y = ax + b$	Simply and easy to use.
Power	$y = ax^b$	The function is called "power" given an increase of x by a factor of t causing an increase of y by the power t^b of t (for $b > 0$).
Quadratic	$y = ax^2 + bx + c$	Used to adjust data when data have minimum and maximum values that can be used as limits of a range of values
Cubic	$y = ax^3 + bx^2 + cx + d$	Used when a minimum or a maximum value can be determined. The selection depends on the context we are analyzing.
Quartic	$y = ax^4 + bx^3 + cx^2 + dx + e$	Used to adjust data when data have minimum and maximum values that can be used as limits of a range of values. When we deal with polynomial models, it is important to consider the significance of the complexity and the precision of the intervals under study.
Exponential	$y = ab^x$ or $y = ae^{kx}$	Has constant percent (relative) rate of change (a constant quotient of two consecutive y values).
Logarithmic	$y = a + b\ln(x)$	If $b > 0$, then the function is increasing and concave down. If $b < 0$, then the function is decreasing and concave up.

Table B.1. Types of linear transformations.

B.2. Linearization process in Empirical Modeling

To propose the best model based on the obtained observations (data values), in EM it is very helpful to linearize a data set, transforming and adjusting a simple model (linearized) based on a transformation processes assuming the simulation of a continuous variable x. Some models can be linearized using the obtained data.

If the functions have some of these forms, the linearization process can be achieved transforming the models considering the relationship with a linear model [1,8]. Keep in mind that if $y = ax^b$, then $ln(y) = ln(a) + bln(x)$; $ln\ y = ln\ a + b\ ln\ x.$; So if y is a power function, $ln(y)$ is a linear function of $ln(x)$.

In modelling certain situations, there is a special interest in some aspects associated with the nature of the values that correspond to the variables under study. Sometimes, the linearization is achieved for a set of variables interacting simultaneously, using a numerical algorithm. One algorithm is called LSM, which is based on the minimization of the corresponding residuals.

Figure B.1 shows the form of a model using x as predictor variable and y as explained or response variable.

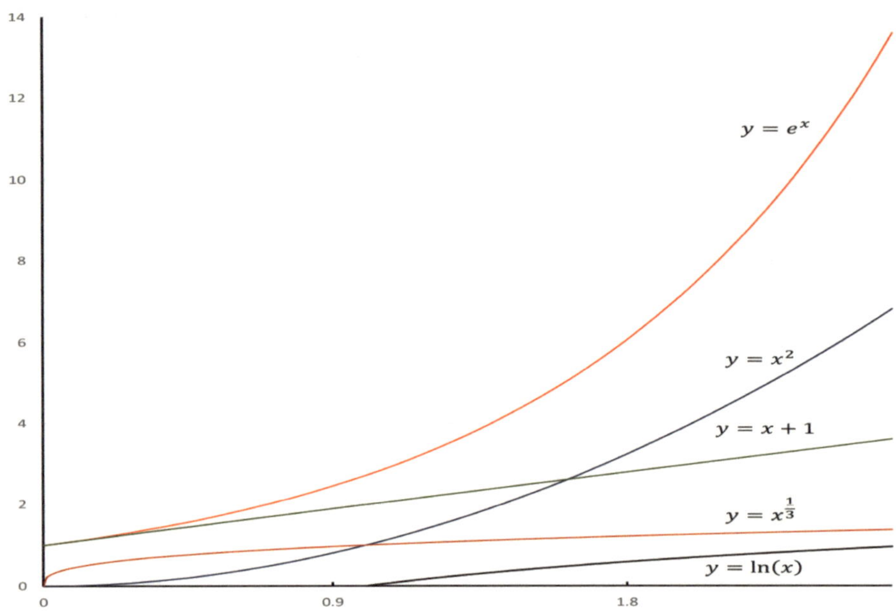

Figure B.1. Several examples of functions.

B.3. Parameters computation when using LSM

In order to compute the parameters a; b; c, …, shown in **Table B.1**, the following general procedure can be adopted. Let's consider the function

$$f(x, p) = \sum_{j=0}^{n} a_j x^j \tag{5}$$

along with the following cost function

$$J(p) = \sum_{i=0}^{m} \left(y_i - f(x_i, p)\right)^2 \tag{6}$$

Where p is the vector of parameters to be determined, i.e., $p = [a_0\, a_1 \ldots a_n]^T$. Then, to determine parameter p, the best fit to the set of data ,(x_i, y_i), corresponds to the parameter p which minimizes the cost function J, and we know from calculus that such a parameter must satisfy:

$$\nabla_p J(p) = 0 \tag{7}$$

Based on this:

$$\sum_{i=1}^{m} x_i^j y_i + \sum_{k=0}^{n} a_k \sum_{i=1}^{m} x_i^{j+k} = 0. \text{ for } j = 0, 1, \cdots, n \tag{8}$$

Since this holds for each $j \in \{0, 1, \cdots, n\}$, then, such a equation can be structured in a convenient way:

$$\begin{bmatrix} m & \sum_{i=1}^{m} x_i & \sum_{i=1}^{m} x_i^2 & \cdots & \sum_{i=1}^{m} x_i^n \\ \sum_{i=1}^{m} x_i & \sum_{i=1}^{m} x_i^2 & \sum_{i=1}^{m} x_i^3 & \cdots & \sum_{i=1}^{m} x_i^{n+1} \\ \vdots & \vdots & \vdots & \ddots & \vdots \\ \sum_{i=1}^{m} x_i^n & \sum_{i=1}^{m} x_i^{n+1} & \sum_{i=1}^{m} x_i^{n+2} & \cdots & \sum_{i=1}^{m} x_i^{2n} \end{bmatrix} \begin{bmatrix} a_0 \\ a_1 \\ \vdots \\ a_n \end{bmatrix} = \begin{bmatrix} \sum_{i=1}^{m} y_i \\ \sum_{i=1}^{m} x_i y_i \\ \vdots \\ \sum_{i=1}^{m} x_i^n y_i \end{bmatrix} \tag{9}$$

Remark

It is clear from the above expression that such an equation can be written as a system of linear equations $Ap=B$. Then, to solve it for a large amount of parameters, several numerical methods can be applied (e.g., Gauss–Seidel, Jacobi, between others).

Author details

Raúl Hernández-Molinar*, Roberto Sarmiento-Rebeles and César F. Méndez-Barrios

*Address all correspondence to: raul.hernandez@uaslp.mx

Autonomous University of San Luis Potosi, San Luis Potos, México

References

[1] Brian Albright. (2010). *Mathematical Modeling with Excel*. Massachussets: Jones and Bartlett Publishers.

[2] Barad M. and Sapir D., (2003). Flexibility in logistics systems-modeling and performance evaluation. *International Journal of Production Economics*, 85, 155–170.

[3] Russell Bertrand. (1961). *The Basic Writings*. George Allen & Unwin Ltd, London.

[4] Parzen Emmanuel. (1979). Nonparametric statistical data modeling. *Journal of the American Association*. 74, 365, 105–120.

[5] Fisher R. A. (1922). On the mathematical foundations of theoretical statistics. *Philosophical Transactions of the Royal Society A*, 222, 309–368.

[6] Tukey J. W. (1993). *Exploratory Data Analysis: Past, Present, and Future*. Princeton: Princeton University.

[7] Oliva R. and Watson N. (2009). Managing functional biases in organizational forecasts: A case study of consensus forecasting in supply chain planning. *Production and Operations Management*, 18, 138–151.

[8] Thompson J. R. (2011) *Empirical Model Building: Data, Models, and Reality*, 2nd Edition. Hoboken: Wiley.

[9] Draper N. R. and Smith H. (1981). *Applied Regression Analysis*. New York: Wiley.

[10] Sen A., and Srivastava M. (1994). *Regression Analysis, Theory, Methods, and Applications*. 2nd Ed. New York: Springer Texts in Statistics.

[11] Weisberg S. (1980). *Applied Linear Regression*. New York: Wiley.

[12] Levenberg K. (1994). A method for the solution of certain nonlinear problems in least squares. *Quarterly of Applied Mathematics*, 2 164–168.

[13] Gilat, A., and Subramaniam V. (2010). *Numerical Methods for Engineers and Scientists*. Columbus: Wiley.

[14] Habib Mamun (2010). Supply chain management: theory and its future perspectives, *International Journal of Business, Management and Social Sciences*, 1: 79--87.

[15] Burgess K., Singh P.J., and Koroglu R. (2006). Supply chain management: a structured literature review and implications for future research. *International Journal of Operations & Production Management*, 26: 703–729.

[16] Fildes R., Goodwin P., Lawrence M., and Nikolopoulos K. (2009). Effective forecasting and judgmental adjustments: an empirical evaluation and strategies for improvement in supply-chain planning. *International Journal of Forecasting*, 25, 3–23.

[17] Sánchez A.M., and Pérez M.P. (2005), Supply chain flexibility and firm performance. *International Journal of Operations & Production Management*, 25, 681–700.

[18] Schutz P., and Tomasgard A., (2009) The impact of flexibility on operational supply chain planning. *International Journal of Production Economics*, doi:10.1016/j.ijpe.2009.11.004.

[19] Wilson R. (2012). 23nd Annual States of Logistics Report. (Research Report). Council of Supply Chain Management Professionals, USA.

Chapter 4

Applied Hydrological Modeling with the Use of Geoinformatics: Theory and Practice

Christos Chalkias, Nikolaos Stathopoulos,
Kleomenis Kalogeropoulos and
Efthimios Karymbalis

Additional information is available at the end of the chapter

http://dx.doi.org/10.5772/62824

Abstract

Water resource management and catchment analysis are crucial aspects of the twenty-first century in hydrological and environmental sciences. Linked directly with studies and research about climate change effects in global resources (e.g., diminution of rainfall dynamic), as well as continuously growing extreme natural phenomena with catastrophic results (e.g., floods and erosion), hydrological modeling has become a key priority in modern academic research goals. On a national or lower administrative level, the need for coping with natural disasters—affecting mainly human life, property, local economy, infrastructure, etc.—and the need to design management plans and projects for sustainable exploitation of natural resources set hydrological modeling in high demand by government organizations and local authorities. Thus, hazard assessment and risk evaluation modeling have become a strategic aim and an extremely useful tool for stakeholders, decision-makers, and scientific community.

Keywords: hydrological modeling, GIS, hydrology, unit hydrograph, floods

1. Introduction

The technological evolution during the last decades, especially in the field of geoinformatics, has offered new opportunities in hydrological modeling. The current efforts are targeted on optimizing existing models (setting some obsolete), evaluating them (with statistical methods, sensitivity analysis, field data, etc.), combining and comparing them, and most important recommending new ones based on original ideas and tools coming from developing technologies, techniques, and sciences. Part of these new technologies, perhaps the most important one, is occupied by Geographical Information Systems (GIS) and Remote Sensing (RS). These technologies stand on the cutting edge of modern geosciences, finding direct implementation in analysis and modeling of natural phenomena and research in key sectors like hydrology.

GIS-based hydrological analysis has a wide range of applications in (true) natural events that demand research, planning, and optimum management. An important aid to implement this methodology is the constantly increasing available free digital data (topographic, morphological, meteorological, land cover, spatially distributed data, etc.), offered by international projects (e.g. CORINE Land use/cover), new technologies such as RS (e.g., SRTM Aster Digital Elevation Model—DEM), national digital databases, and many other available sources. These data are continuously improving in volume, reliability, and spatial detail due to technological evolution, creating thus important databases (significant time series, spatial resolution, etc.) that along with freeware GIS software (e.g., QGIS and HEC-RAS) reduce cost, time, and improve efficacy in hydrological modeling.

Following not only new scientific trends but also contemporary demands and perspectives, the need for interdisciplinary approaches, in modeling natural processes and phenomena, is gaining more and more ground. For example, modeling runoff in a catchment via GIS can be implemented by a combination of satellite data, in situ measurements, time series data, etc., demanding thus a spherical perception of the study subject (e.g., hydrographic network characteristics, rainfall dynamic, and terrain characteristics) by combining various disciplines such as hydrology, geology, geomorphology, and hydrometeorology. Furthermore, the GIS-based modeling of natural processes requires a minimum understanding of data nature and limitations and processing of algorithms used by the software not only in order to implement the methodology but also to distinguish modeling errors and validate the analysis.

2. Literature review[1]

Novel environmental challenges have placed water resources management in high academic and research interest. Climate changes throughout the last decades, resulting in temperature augmentation, rainfall volume diminution, desertification, etc., and on the other hand in extreme events such as storms, flooding, landslides and soil erosion, threaten human lives and infrastructures. This constantly forming and alternating environmental regime has upgraded the need for scientific research on relevant disciplines like hydrology. Key goals of this effort are better methodological efficiency, optimum database management (as data volume is continually multiplying and demanding time-consuming data mining) and, more importantly, state-of-the-art modeling, as the understanding and forecasting of an event or a phenomenon are of utmost importance nowadays. Modern technologies based on Geoinformatics (e.g., GIS and RS, respectively) play a crucial role in this ongoing attempt.

[1] It must be mentioned that all referred and described publications were selected based, mostly, on their citations in an attempt to quote the ones with the highest impact in the disciplines discussed in this chapter. For this purpose Scopus citation index was used.

http://dx.doi.org/10.5772/62824

2.1. Applied hydrological modeling during 1970s

Many researchers have published (and keep publishing) their work on hydrological issues throughout the years, contributing to literature volume rise concerning this topic and scientific knowledge. A general publications recursion and description over the last 45 years in hydrological references could start with Nash et al. and their series of papers in 1970 in *Journal of Hydrology*. Nash and Sutcliffe [1] attempted to state the need for a more efficient transition from classical hydrology to applied hydrology. In the first part of their publication series, they tried to propose a number of principles for river flow forecasting through conceptual models, which were put to a test in their second and third parts by applying these principles in two case studies in Brosna Catchment at Ferbane [2] and Ray Catchment at Grendon Underwood [3].

As hydrological modeling started to flourish in scientific research, in the years that followed, many notable studies came to light. Among them, Beven's and Kirkby's work [4] was distinctive as they developed a hydrological forecasting model that combined the important distributed effects of channel network topology and dynamic contributing areas with the advantages of simple lumped parameter basin models. In the same year, Rodriguez-Iturbe and Valdes [5] attempted a unifying synthesis of the hydrological response of a catchment to surface runoff, by linking the instantaneous unit hydrograph (IUH) with the geomorphologic parameters of a basin. Closing the decade as it started, Kitanidis and Bras followed Nash and his colleagues (their work 10 years earlier) in setting a conceptual hydrological model for real-time short-term forecasts of river flows. Their first paper refers to an uncertainty analysis of the model, while the second to its applications and results [6, 7].

2.2. *Applied hydrological modeling during 1980s*

During the 1980s new ideas were published, establishing for good the digital era in hydrological modeling, as well as ones relevant to the rising need for evaluation and improvement of physically based models. In 1984, O'Callaghan et al. [8] carried forward to the scientific community their method for extracting drainage networks from digital elevation data, and 5 years later, Hutchinson [9] proposed a new procedure (the ANUDEM algorithm) for gridding elevation and stream line data. In the years between, and specifically in 1986, the Danish Hydraulic Institute along with the British Institute of Hydrology and SOGREAH (France) published their work on "Systeme Hydrologique Europeen" (SHE). This model was developed under the perception that conventional rainfall/runoff models are inappropriate to many demanding hydrological problems, especially those related to the impact of man's activities on land-use change and water quality, and that only through the use of models which have a physical basis and allow for spatial variations within a catchment can these problems be tackled. This work was described in two chapters in *Journal of Hydrology*, where the first covered the evolution and general philosophy and the second the structure of the model [10, 11]. At the end of the decade, Beven expressed his criticism about problems in the application of physically based models for practical prediction in hydrology, focusing on limitations and lack of theory in specific aspects, practical constraints, and dimensionality issues [12].

2.3. *Applied hydrological modeling during 1990s*

In the years between 1990 and 2000, there is a research outburst concerning hydrological modeling. The studies published in this period cover a wide range of topics referring either directly or indirectly to the discipline of hydrology. Environmental, climatic, and natural hazard issues became extremely important this decade (fact that continued if not increased until today), boosting scientists to direct their interests in aspects such as hydrological modeling interaction with soil erosion, landslides, and vegetation. Attempting a brief overview over these matters, a small number of relevant publications will be cited in the following paragraphs.

Maidment proposed a methodology based on GIS raster structure in order to extract a spatially distributed single hydrograph by calculating flow velocities for each cell in the study area. Subsequently, this flow velocity layer is calculated by the influx time of the water in each cell, at the river mouth, by dividing the flow length to velocity. Then, the isochronous curves are constructed (equal confluency time) together with the time-area chart (catchment surface which reflects the increasing extent of the basin that contributes to runoff through time). The unit hydrograph of the basin results from the slope of cumulative runoff surface. The velocity field is permanent, meaning that it is constant over time throughout the duration of the precipitation [13].

Daly et al. [14] proposed Precipitation-elevation Regressions on Independent Slopes Model (PRISM) trying to meet the demand for climatological precipitation fields on a regular grid, as ecological and hydrological models became increasingly linked to GIS that spatially represent and manipulate model output. Montgomery and his colleagues described their model for the topographic influence on shallow landslide initiation, by coupling digital terrain data with near-surface through flow and slope stability models. More specifically, they used "TOPOG" hydrological model in order to predict the degree of soil saturation in response to a steady-state rainfall for topographic elements defined by the intersection of contours and flow tube boundaries, which was later used by the slope stability component to analyze the stability of each topographic element for the case of cohesionless soils of spatially constant thickness and saturated conductivity [15, 16]. In parallel, Wigmosta et al. [17] presented their distributed hydrology—vegetation model that included canopy interception, evaporation, transpiration, and snow accumulation and melt, as well as runoff generation via the saturation excess mechanisms.

Sellers et al. [18] completed the revision of their first model Simple Biosphere ("SiB") model creating the new edition "SiB2", which belongs to a wider group of models that are called General Circulation Models (Atmospheric—"GSMs"). "SiB2" includes canopy photosynthesis—conductance model, use of satellite data to describe the vegetation phenology, a hydrological submodel for describing baseflows and calculate interlayer exchanges within the soil profile, and other tools covering aspects like snowmelt [19]. Morgan et al. [20] published European Soil Erosion Model ("EUROSEM"), which is a dynamic distributed model, able to simulate

http://dx.doi.org/10.5772/62824

sediment transport, erosion, and deposition over the land surface and its outputs include total runoff, total soil loss, storm hydrograph, and storm sediment graph.

Many researchers have applied the spatially distributed unit hydrograph with spatially variable rainfall, included losses of rain by using the method of curve numbers (Curve Number, USDA), which is particularly suitable for use in a GIS environment, resulting in successful simulated hydrographs that had arisen from actual measurements [21].

In 2000, Iverson tried via a mathematical model to evaluate the effects of rainfall infiltration on landslide occurrence, timing, depth, and acceleration in diverse situations [22]. Finally, the same year, Vörösmarty et al. issued a critical review on global water resources arguing on their vulnerability from climate change and population. The point of views that they expressed was derived by co-evaluation, analysis, and combination of climate model outputs, water budgets, and socioeconomic information along digitized river networks. In few words, they resulted in the opinion that a large proportion of the world's population is currently experiencing water stress and that rising water demands greatly outweigh greenhouse warming in defining the state of global water systems to 2025. They also stated that the consideration of direct human impacts on global water supply remains a poorly articulated but potentially important facet of the larger global change question [23]. These ideas strengthened the need for hydrological research and sustainable management of water resources, setting thus hydrological modeling as an important priority, and laid the carpet for the 21st century's scientific goals.

Focusing purely on hydrological modeling and analysis, during the decade 1990–2000, it is highly noticeable that new technologies begin to occupy significant space in this field. For example, RS techniques start to define their part as a useful, modern, and continuously evolving scientific trend in environmental sciences and therefore, in hydrology. In short reference, Houser et al. [24] wrote their paper on integrating soil moisture RS and hydrological modeling, while Jackson et al. [25] used microwave radiometry in an attempt to map soil moisture in regional scales. Another parallel trend, on hydrological modeling, these years was neural network modeling. Dawson and Wilby made their approach to rainfall—runoff modeling via Artificial Neural Networks (ANN) [26, 27], and Govindaraju [28, 29] followed them in 2000 with his two papers about ANN in hydrology.

Nevertheless, the most distinctive and influential research topic of 1990s was the coupling of Digital Elevation Model (DEMs) analysis and raster-based hydrological modeling, which consolidated the use of GIS in hydrology. In 1991, there were many authors that directed their interests toward raster modeling. Tarboton et al. [30] wrote about the extraction of channel networks from digital elevation data, Moore et al. [31] published a review on hydrological, geomorphological, and biological applications through digital terrain modeling, Quinn et al. [32] attempted a prediction of hillslope flow paths using DEMs, and finally, Fairfield and Leymarie [33] worked on deriving drainage networks from grid DEMs. Three years later, Zhang and Montgomery examined the effect of DEM's grid size in landscape representation and hydrological simulations [16], and Tarboton [34] proposed a new method for the determination of flow directions and upslope areas in grid DEMs. Bates and De Roo [35] closed the century with their raster-based model for flood inundation simulation.

2.4. *Hydrological modeling during the period 2001–2015*

The 21st century started with the place and significance of GIS, RS, and other modern technologies in hydrological modeling well established. New scientists targeted in developing new ideas based on the previous works and tools. Free software packages were developed and distributed, huge global digital data banks were created and various research projects took place. The evolution and revolution of hydrological modeling via modern technologies still flourish, finding constantly new applications, meeting continuously growing demands, and inviting more and more new scientists to work on this field. In the following paragraphs, a short literature review of the last 15 years will be presented, starting with a brief reference on hydrological modeling in general and followed by a wider review on the main topic of this chapter.

Beven continued his critical reviews on hydrological modeling with a discussion concerning the problems of distributed models [36]. In the same period, Dawson and Wilby applied ANN, a highly emerging field of research, for rainfall-runoff modeling and flood forecasting [27]. Simultaneously, Thiemann et al. coped with the problem of uncertainty of hydrological modeling, which is the compound effect of the parameter, data, and structural uncertainties associated with the applied model. They presented the framework for a Bayesian recursive estimation approach to hydrological prediction that can be used for simultaneous parameter estimation and prediction in an operational setting [37]. A similar attempt was made a few years later by Ajami et al. [38] with their integrated hydrological Bayesian multimodel combination framework, which also tried to confront the uncertainties in hydrological predictions.

As new ideas and techniques dominate the field, Hock [39] approached a different aspect of hydrological modeling, with direct reference on environmental and climate change. It was none other than temperature index snow or ice melt modeling. Also, Döll et al. expressed their interest on global environmental issues by introducing Water GAP Global Hydrology Model (WGHM), which computes surface runoff, groundwater recharge, and river discharge at a spatial resolution of 0.5 and is a submodel of the global water use and availability model WaterGAP 2, which was also introduced in the same year [40, 41].

One of the most innovative ideas published in 2004 was that of Nayak et al. [42], concerning the combination of ANN and fuzzy logic approaches, creating thus a neuro—fuzzy hybrid computing technique for modeling hydrological time series. Finally, the Distributed Model Intercomparison Project (DMIP) was selected as a last reference for 2004, due to its distinctive concept, as it was formulated as a broad comparison of many distributed models among themselves and to a lumped model used for operational river forecasting in the US [43].

Closing the general reference on hydrological modeling, it would be inconsiderate not to mention Soil and Water Assessment Tool (SWAT), which is a conceptual, continuous time model that was developed in the early 1990s to assist water resource managers in assessing the impact of management and climate on water supplies and nonpoint source pollution in watersheds and large river basins. This tool was developed further in the 21st century (and keeps developing), and many research studies were based on its application. Some of the most

http://dx.doi.org/10.5772/62824

indicative ones are the papers by Arnold and Fohrer [44], by Abbaspour et al. [45], by Kalogeropoulos et al. [46], as well as by Kalogeropoulos and Chalkias [47]. The first refers to SWAT2000 and its capabilities and research opportunities in applied watershed modeling, while the second concerns an application of the model on hydrology and water quality in the prealpine/Alpine Thur watershed. The third one was the developing of a methodology of water resources exploitation, with the potential of creating small mountainous and upland reservoirs, by coupling hydrological analysis and SWAT model. The fourth one was an attempt of hydrological modeling incorporating SWAT model in a GIS environment in order to exam various scenarios of climate change in a Mediterranean catchment. Equally important are the RS-based approaches targeting hydrological—environmental modeling. Among the most important ones is NASA's modern-era retrospective analysis for research and applications (MERRA), the history of which as well as its contemporary development and applications are sufficiently described [48]. SWAT and other similar models along with RS is highly linked and coupled with GIS, as shown below.

2.5. *GIS and hydrological modeling, 2001–2015*

The last part of this literature review aims at identifying the most influential publications of the last 15 years, about empirical hydrological modeling and GIS integration.

In 2001, Weng [49] developed a methodology to relate urban growth studies to distributed hydrological models using an integrated approach of RS and GIS. Following a similar concept, Fortin et al. [50] proposed HYDROTEL, a distributed watershed hydrological model compatible with RS and GIS. US Environmental Protection Agency Office of Water developed Better Assessment Science Integrating Point and Nonpoint Sources (BASINS) system, which integrates GIS, watershed tools, and SWAT model [51]. In parallel, in order to analyze land cover changes, a landscape assessment tool was developed by using a GIS that automates the parameterization of the SWAT and KINEmatic Runoff and EROSion (KINEROS) hydrological models [52]. The first three years of the century closed with Liu et al. [53] proposing a GIS-based diffusive transport approach for the determination of rainfall runoff response and flood routing through a catchment, and with Al-Sabhan et al. [54], introducing a real-time hydrological model for flood prediction using GIS and the World Wide Web. Finally, one of the most interesting studies of 2003 was the work of Huggel et al. [55], which proposes a modeling approach, which takes into account the current evolution of the glacial environment and satisfies a robust first-order assessment of hazards from glacier-lake outbursts in the southern Swiss Alps.

In the next three years, a lot of significant papers were published. Lan et al. [56] used hydrological modeling and GIS for spatial analysis and prediction of landslide hazard in the Xiaojiang watershed, Yunnan, China. During the same year, a grid or cell-based process-oriented distributed rainfall-runoff model, capable of handling the catchment heterogeneity in terms of distributed information on landuse, slope, soil, and rainfall, was developed and applied to isolated storm events in several catchments by Jain et al. [57]. Knebl et al. [58] published their work on regional scale flood modeling that integrates NEXRAD Level III rainfall, GIS, and hydrological model HEC-HMS/RAS, applied on San Antonio River Basin in

Central Texas, USA, for a specific storm event. Furthermore, among the most distinguished papers of 2005 was the study of Kyoung et al. [59] in which two digital filter-based separation modules, the BFLOW and Eckhardt filters, were incorporated into the Web-based Hydrograph Analysis Tool (WHAT) system, whose Web GIS version accesses and uses US Geological Survey (USGS) daily streamflow data from the USGS web server. Jia et al. [60] developed the WEP-L, a physically based distributed hydrological model, which couples simulations of natural hydrological and water use processes, with the aid of RS data and GIS techniques. At the same time, Olivera et al. [61] presented ArcGIS-SWAT, a geodata model and GIS interface for the SWAT. The final reference for 2006 concerns the work of Wolski et al. [62] on modeling of the flooding in the Okavango Delta, Botswana, using a hybrid reservoir-GIS model, which is a semidistributed and semiconceptual approach.

Melesse and Graham proposed a GIS-based model on calculating the routing time. They perceived the flow within the basin into two major types of flow: the flow into the main river channel and the overland flow (flow onto the slopes of the catchment). Here, the flow time for each cell is the sum of the flow times of all the cells along the path of the water (from each cell until the mouth of the catchment). Instead of the unit hydrograph, they proposed the calculation of a direct flood hydrograph, resulting directly from the sum of the volumetric flow rates of all the confluent cells at each time step. This model was a fixed time spatially distributed direct hydrograph approach [63].

The need to exploit hydrological models for researching various environmental aspects and hazards lead Pandey et al. [64] on an attempt to identify the critical erosion prone areas of Karso watershed of Hazaribagh, Jharkhand, in India, using Universal Soil Loss Equation (USLE), RS technology, and GIS technologies. Simultaneously, Miller et al. [65] presented an open-source toolkit for distributed hydrological modeling at multiple scales called the Automated Geospatial Watershed Assessment (AGWA) tool, which uses commonly available GIS data layers to fully parameterize, execute, and visualize results from both the SWAT and Kinematic Runoff and Erosion model (KINEROS2). In 2008, an approach for groundwater vulnerability assessment (covering thus another sector of hydrology) in shallow aquifer in Aligarh, India, was made by Rahman [66], using a GIS-based DRASTIC model. Jonkman et al. [67] tried to cope with the problem of flood damage in the Netherlands, by integrating hydrodynamic and economic modeling via GIS, offering thus a new approach and perspective in the analysis of this natural phenomenon. During 2009, various interesting papers were published. Among them the studies of Maksimovic et al. [68], Chen et al. [69], Milewski et al. [70], and Sheikh et al. [71] stood out. The first two papers dealt with urban flooding via GIS modeling combining various techniques, tools and data, like high-resolution Digital Elevation Model data collected by the LiDAR technique and GIS-based urban flood inundation model (GUFIM), respectively. The third paper concerns applied methodologies for rainfall-runoff and groundwater recharge computations that heavily rely on observations extracted from a wide-range of global RS datasets (TRMM, SSM/I, Landsat TM, AVHRR, AMSR-E, and ASTER), using the arid Sinai Peninsula and the Eastern Desert of Egypt as test sites, while the fourth one introduced Bridge Event and Continuous Hydrological (BEACH) model (developed in GIS), used for predicting soil moisture.

Du et al. [72] proposed a spatially distributed model similar with the model of Melesse and Graham [63], but they took into account the temporal variability. The improvement relates to the calculation of the variation of flow time in each cell, due to the velocity variance, regarding the uneven distribution of rainfall over time. This model also incorporated the rainfall losses by using the curve number methodology (Soil Conservation Service [73]). This model was named time variant spatially distributed direct hydrograph.

At the end of the decade, Van der Knijff et al. [74], described the spatially distributed LISFLOOD model, which is a hydrological model specifically developed for the simulation of hydrological processes in large European river basins.

As flood management became more and more important due to climate change and other environmental and human factors, many researchers pointed their work toward these issues. In this frame, Rozalis et al. [75] used an uncalibrated hydrological model and radar rainfall data for flash flood prediction in a Mediterranean watershed. Also in 2010, Kourgialas et al. [76] published a very interesting case study about Koiliaris River Basin, located east of the city of Chania on the island of Crete in Greece, proposing an integrated framework for the hydrological simulation of this complex geomorphological river basin that includes a two-part Maillet Karstic model, a GIS-based Energy Budget Snow Melt model, an empirical karstic channel model and the Hydrological Simulation Program—FORTRAN (HSPF) model. In the year that followed, Paiva et al. [77] presented a large-scale hydrological model with a full one-dimensional hydrodynamic module to calculate flow propagation on a complex river network, while Lei et al. [78] developed an efficient and cost-effective distributed hydrological modeling tool (MWEasyDHM) based on open-source MapWindow GIS. Furthermore, Fugura et al. [79] coupled hydrodynamic simulation with a well-developed digital surface and terrain model (DEM), derived by aerial photogrammetry, to map flood extent in Kuala Lumpur, Malaysia. Kia et al. [80] developed a flood model, using various flood causative factors, ANN techniques, and GIS to model and simulate flood-prone areas in the southern part of Peninsular Malaysia. Sarhadi et al. linked GIS techniques (HEC-GeoRAS, IRS-P6 satellite images, etc.) with frequency analysis, aiming at probabilistic flood inundation mapping of ungauged rivers and more specifically of the Halilrud basin and Jiroft city in southeastern Iran, which were selected as an example of hazardous regions [81].

Despite the significant volume of previous research, the publication list in this topic is still increasing. Lopez–Vicente et al., used the modified version of the revised Morgan, Morgan and Finney (RMMF) model to predict the hydrological connectivity and the rates of soil erosion under four different scenarios of land uses and land abandonment along with GIS in the Estanque de Arriba catchment (Spanish Pre-Pyrenees) [82]. Paiva et al. [83] published their validation work for the implementation of MGB-IPH hydrological model, which uses full Saint Venant equations, a simple storage model for flood inundation and GIS-based algorithms to extract model parameters from digital elevation models, on large-scale hydrological modeling in the Amazon and specifically in the Solimões River basin. Tehrany et al. [84] proposed a novel methodology for flood susceptibility mapping, where weights-of-evidence (WoE) model was utilized first to assess the impact of classes of each conditioning factor on flooding through bivariate statistical analysis (BSA) and then, these factors were reclassified using the acquired weights and entered into the support vector machine (SVM) model to evaluate the correlation between flood occurrence and each conditioning factor. Another published novel idea of the year was that of Formetta et al. [85], who described the structure of JGrass-NewAge: a system for hydrological forecasting and modeling of water resources at the basin scale. Furthermore, among the published papers of 2014, the integration of RS and GIS occupies a rather special place, with the most influential works on this topic. Chen et al. [86] developed a methodology for regional estimates of potential floodwater retention under floodplain inundation, from ecologically significant flood return periods, by coupling RS and GIS technologies with spatial hydrological modeling. Mahmoud [87] estimated the potential runoff coefficient (PRC), using GIS, based on the area's hydrologic soil group (HSG), land use, slope, and determined the runoff volume in Egypt. Finally, Fiorillo et al. [88], published a model for simulating recharge processes of karst massifs and Krysanova et al. [89] used Soil and Water Integrated Model (SWIM) to model climate and land-use change impacts (four different application studies were made and analyzed). Both research works couple GIS and hydrological modeling.

In conclusion, from the references presented above, it can be easily deduced that hydrological modeling occupies a distinguished place in environmental modeling and research. The latest trends in the field are RS techniques and GIS coupled with hydrological modeling. The development and application of this coupling is expected to flourish the following years in scientific research.

3. Applied hydrological modeling—An empirical paradigm

3.1. A general description of the methodology

As mentioned earlier, GIS-based hydrological analysis has a very wide variety of applications in natural events and natural disasters. This part of the chapter intends to highlight the contribution of GIS in hydrological analysis and simulation by presenting an empirical analysis.

The basic aim of this simulation is to estimate the peak flood discharge, derived by an extreme rainfall event, as well as the critical time to reach this peak right after the rainfall peak. In order to do that, a synthetic Unit Hydrograph (UH) is obtained by estimating the time-area curve. The curve (histogram) of time-area shows the spatiotemporal relationship during time at which water flows within the basin. This curve can be expressed with a reclassification of time concentration at specific time intervals. These time periods are distinguished by isochrones. These are the lines within the catchment where runoff has the same travel time to reach the outlet of the basin.

According to the theory of the UH, the duration of the flood is the same for any given amount of active rainfall duration, while the ordinates of the hydrograph on the joint duration (time base flood) is directly proportional to the amount of rain (Chow et al., 1988). Thus, the discharge at the outlet of the basin is resulting from the superposition (addition) of instantaneous UH produced by active rain at each time step. UHs in hydrological practice are exported with numerical techniques from observed hydrographs. Many scientists have used GIS technology in order to construct rainfall-runoff model for UH attainment [13, 21, 63, 72].

In order to estimate the magnitude of a flood, a routing model was designed in a GIS context [63, 72, 90, 91]. The choice of the specific model was based mainly on its ability to be created entirely in a GIS environment. Accordingly, this model is very flexible to changes and connection with other models. Also, it is expandable, and it can be easily used in different areas.

3.2. The proposed method: data and methods

3.2.1. Data

The basic concept of the simulation is the runoff analysis in a GIS environment given a specific storm. The initiate data which is needed for this simulation is

3.2.1.1. The rainfall

The model can incorporate various types of rainfall data. More specifically, data derived by rainfall stations can be used. In this case, the use of them depends on the number of meteorological gauge stations. So, for example, if there is only one rainfall station in the river basin (i.e., the study area), the rain data is entered into the model (the simulation) as cumulative rainfall (single number). The distribution of rainfall is used after the modeling to construct the flood hydrograph. This simulation is taking into account only the time distribution of the rainfall (time modeling).

If the study area has more than one meteorological gauge stations, then the best way to handle all the rainfall data is to proceed to the tessellation of the data, e.g., with the creation of Voronoi (Thiessen polygons) geometries. In this way, the simulation is taking into account, besides time, the spatial context of the rainfall distribution (semispatiotemporal modeling).

Nowadays, the use of radar for record rainfall, or the use of data that are provided by Atmospheric Simulation Model, has provided the ability to incorporate in the hydrological modeling both the spatial and temporal variation of rainfall (spatiotemporal modeling).

In each case, the best way to simplify the hydrological modeling is to modify the total rainfall in terms of the part of rainfall which finally becomes surface runoff (excess rainfall). This data can be extracted from Atmospheric Simulation (the rainfall grid values can be only the excess rainfall). Otherwise, techniques such as Curve Numbers CN can be established in order to be used as a layer in the process of simulation [72].

Figure 1 presents the most common types of rainfall data which can be used in the model. **Figure 1a** shows a study area which is covered from only one rain station. **Figure 1b** presents a study area which is covered from many rain gauge stations (that is why the Thiessen polygons are used), and **Figure 1c** shows six different raster presentation of a 3-h cumulative rainfall (each one) and all together (in a row) cover the entire flood event.

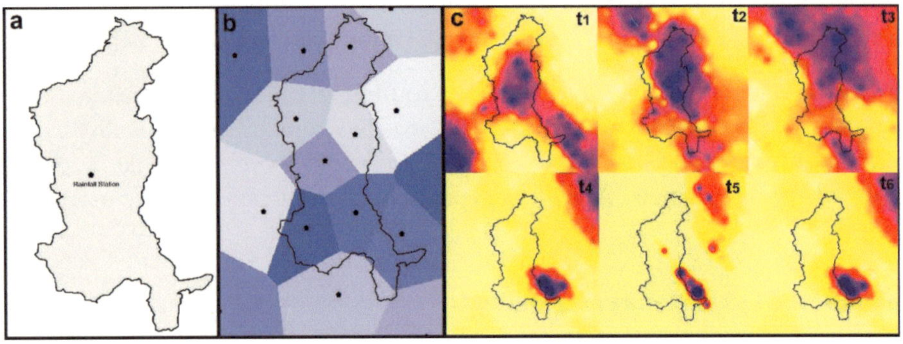

Figure 1. (a) One weather station—time modeling, (b) many weather stations—semi-spatiotemporal modeling (dots represents meteorological stations), (c) use of atmospheric simulation data—spatiotemporal modeling (t_1–t_6 are time snapshots of 3-h cumulative rainfall, blue color indicate high values of cumulative rainfall & yellow color indicate low values of cumulative rainfall).

3.2.1.2. A Manning's n roughness coefficient layer

In order to perform the simulation a Manning's roughness coefficient layer is needed. The construction of such a layer requires a land use/land cover (LULC) map of the study area.

Each type of LULC is assigned to Manning's roughness coefficient values using suitable lookup tables like the one in **Table 1** (for more details see reference [92]).

Description	**Manning's n**
Forest/Forest mixed	0.1
Urban/Urban mixed	0.015
Pasture/Pasture mixed	0.03
Permant Crop/Permant crop mixed	0.035
Arable Crop/Arable crop mixed	0.03
Olive/Olive mixed	0.15
Vineyard/Vineyard mixed	0.05

Table 1. Lookup table to assign Manning's roughness coefficient values to LULC.

After pairing the values of each LULC type to Manning's *n* values, the roughness coefficient layer (grid) is constructed.

3.2.1.3. A Digital Elevation Model (DEM)

The digital elevation models have been used, during the last decades along with the development of GIS, in order to derive hydrological and hydro-geomorphological properties such as streams, basins, flow direction, flow accumulation, flow length, and stream order. Nowadays, the development in satellite technology provides very high accuracy for remotely sensed data in terms of landscape topography. Alternatively, data generated from digitization of topographic maps can be used after applying the suitable algorithms in order to create a DEM, e.g., the algorithm ANUDEM.[93]. This specific algorithm produces a coherent grid which maintains the integrity of the topography [94]. Another way of constructing DEM is to use data derived from the use of Laser Scanners. The elevation point cloud is converted to Triangulated Irregular Network (TIN) and then is converted to DEM.

In GIS-based hydrological analysis, the use of DEM is exceptional and of critical importance. The cell size of a DEM largely determines the accuracy of the analysis that is carried out each time.

3.2.2. *The methodology*

The methodology which is presented in this paradigm is actually based on the estimation of concentration time in order to construct a layer of isochrones. Accordingly, calculations were carried out for flow time within the basin, both for channel and overland flow. In order to discrete these two types of water flow, a suitable threshold on flow accumulation must be selected. This can be done by several iterations until the stream layer reflect reality. Hence, the two types of flow are separated, and it also results in drainage network determination and mapping. As mentioned before, the topography of the land surface (expressed by a DEM) is one of the most fundamental elements for this simulation. Thus, DEM construction and analysis is the first step in order to execute the current rainfall-runoff model. There are various derivatives from the hydrological analysis of a DEM such as the slope (surface analysis), flow direction, flow accumulation, and flow length (hydrological analysis).

By extracting the flow accumulation layer (from the above DEM analysis), the discharge within the channel (Q_{ch} in m^3/s) of the river is calculated according to Eq 1:

$$Q_{ch} = \frac{R \times Flow.accumulation \times cell.size^2}{T_R} \tag{1}$$

where R is the amount of rainfall (in meters) and T_R is the duration of rainfall (in seconds). If the rainfall comes from only one meteorological station, R is actually a number which represents the amount of rainfall throughout the duration of the event. If the rainfall comes from several gauge stations, R is a grid layer which corresponds to closest gauge station. Lastly, if the rainfall comes from several grid layers which represent the spatiotemporal distribution of the rain, the discharge within the channel must be calculated as many times as the number of the separate grids. Then, these grids are added to give the total discharge within the river network.

The velocity of the water within the channel (V_c in m/s) can be estimated according to the combination of Manning's equation with the continuity equation by using the following Eq 2:

$$V_c = K \times S_0^{3/8} \times Q_{ch}^{1/4} \times n^{-3/4} \quad (2)$$

Where $S_0^{3/8}$ is the surface slope (m/m), Q is the cumulative discharge (m^3/s) which is calculated above, and n is the Manning's roughness coefficient. K is a coefficient that is determined after the calibration of the model and corrects the simulation errors of slope and n. Measurements of real discharge (Q) are very helpful and highly desirable in order to calibrate the model. The value "1" of K is a good starting point for ungauged basins.

Likewise, the overland flow velocity (V_0 in m) can be estimated according to Eq 3:

$$V_c = S_0^{3/8} \times l^{2/5} \times i_e^{2/5} \times n^{-3/5} \quad (3)$$

where S_0 is the surface slope (m/m), l is the length of the slope (m), i_e is the vertical net incoming flux (m/s), and n is the Manning's roughness coefficient. The combination of the above two types of velocities provides the final velocity, since the final velocity is calculated for each cell off the basin (using conditional algorithms).

The travel time (T in s) in each cell was computed from the travel distance using as a weight raster the $1/V$ grid as illustrated by Eq 4:

$$T = Flow.Length \times \frac{1}{V} \quad (4)$$

All the above equations can be calculated with the use of map algebra in a GIS software package. Map Algebra is a language that defines a syntax for combining map themes by applying mathematical operations and analytical functions to create new map themes. In a map algebra expression, the operators are a combination of mathematical, logical, or Boolean operators (+, >, AND, tan, etc.), and spatial analysis functions (slope, shortest path, spline, etc), and the operands are spatial data and numbers.

Finally, in order to estimate the flow time and isochrones (i.e., curves that connect areas of the basin where the runoff needs the same time to reach the exit of the basin), it is necessary to reclassify the values of travel time T.

The flow chart of the methodology is presented in **Figure 2**.

http://dx.doi.org/10.5772/62824

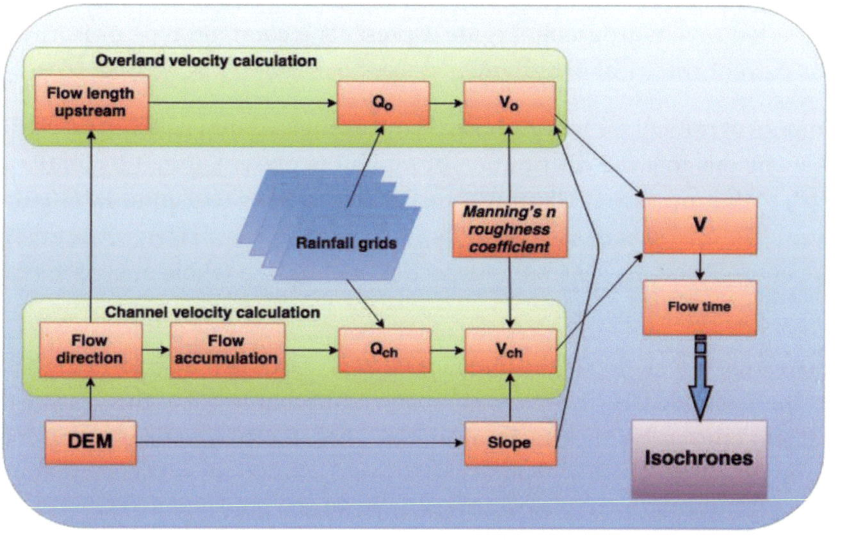

Figure 2. The flow chart of the methodology.

3.3. Results

The time-area unit hydrograph theory, as it known, inaugurates a specific association between the travel time *T* and a part of the upper catchment that may contribute runoff during this travel time *T*. The area which is closest to the catchment outlet will contribute to the runoff hydrograph sooner than the other areas which are on the catchment boundary. This method indicates that the catchment is divided into areas of approximately travel time (isochrones).

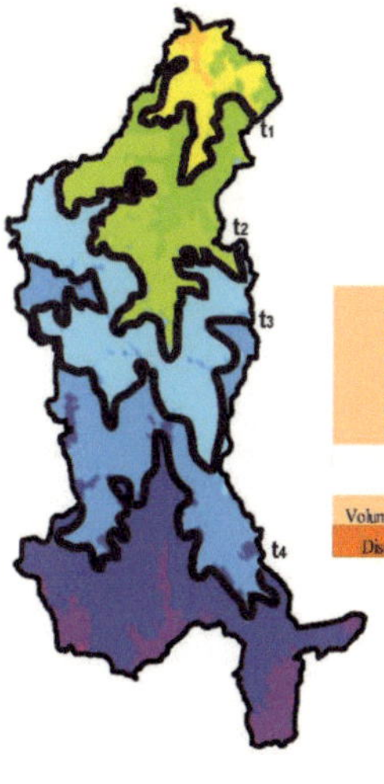

Flow time (isochrones)			Area	(km^2)
t1	→	1h	A_{t01}	3.2
t2	→	2h	A_{t12}	6.3
t3	→	3h	A_{t23}	8.1
t4	→	4h	A_{t34}	6.7
			A_{t4-}	9.4

	R1	R2	R3	R4	R5	R6	← snapshots of 3-hour cumulative rainfall
Area (m^2)	0.01	0.025	0.005	0.01	0.015	0.007	← Rainfall in meters
3200000	32000	80000	16000	32000	48000	22400	
6300000	63000	157500	31500	63000	94500	44100	
8100000	81000	202500	40500	81000	121500	56700	
6700000	67000	167500	33500	67000	100500	46900	
9400000	94000	235000	47000	94000	141000	65800	

	Palm 1	Palm 2	Palm 3	Palm 4	Palm 5	Palm 6	Palm 7	Palm 8	Palm 9	Palm 10
Volume of water (m^3)	32000	143000	254500	333000	413000	466400	279600	251200	187900	65800
Discharge (m^3/s)	26.6667	119.167	212.083	277.5	344.167	388.667	233	209.333	156.583	54.8333

Figure 3. Reclassified travel time (time zones, isochrones).

These lines of equal travel time are known as isochrones. Hence, the time-area histogram is actually converted to a hydrograph. **Figure 3** presents a common type of isochrones for the needs of this current empirical paradigm.

The total amount of rainfall for the examined flood event is 72 mm (0.072 m) within 18 h. From **Figure 3** it is obvious that the distribution of rainfall is presented in 3-h cumulative rainfall snapshots (R_1 = 10 mm, R_2 = 0.025 mm, R_3 = 0.005 mm, R_4 = 0.01 mm, R_5 = 0.015 mm, and R_6 = 0.007 mm). The area of each time zone (0 t_1, t_1 t_2, t_2 t_3, t_3 t_4, t_4 end) is A_1 = 3.2 km^2, A_2 = 6.3 km^2, A_3 = 8.1 km^2, A_4 = 6.7 km^2, A_5 = 9.4 km^2, respectively (thus, the whole area of the catchment is 33.7 km^2).

The main goal is the calculation of the discharge that is reaching the outlet of the basin in order to construct the synthetic UH (the so-called "palm of discharge"). For this reason, the amount of water that falls onto each time zone is calculated. Thus, for the first time zone (t_1), the amount of water during the first 3 h is $V_{11} = R_1{*}A1$ = 0.01 m*3,200,000 m^2 = 32,000 m^3, for the second time zone (t_2) is $V_{21} = R_2{*}A_1$ = 0.025 m*6,300,000 m^2 = 80,000 m^3, etc.

The next step is the calculation of the total volume for each palm of water discharge that reaches the outlet of the basin. Thus, the volume of the first palm is $V_{palm1} = V_{11}$ = 32,000 m^3 (the first purple cell in **Figure 3**), the volume of the second palm is $V_{palm}2 = V21 + V12$ = 80,000 m^3 + 63,000 m^3 = 143,000 m^3 (the sum of the first red cells in **Figure 3**) etc.

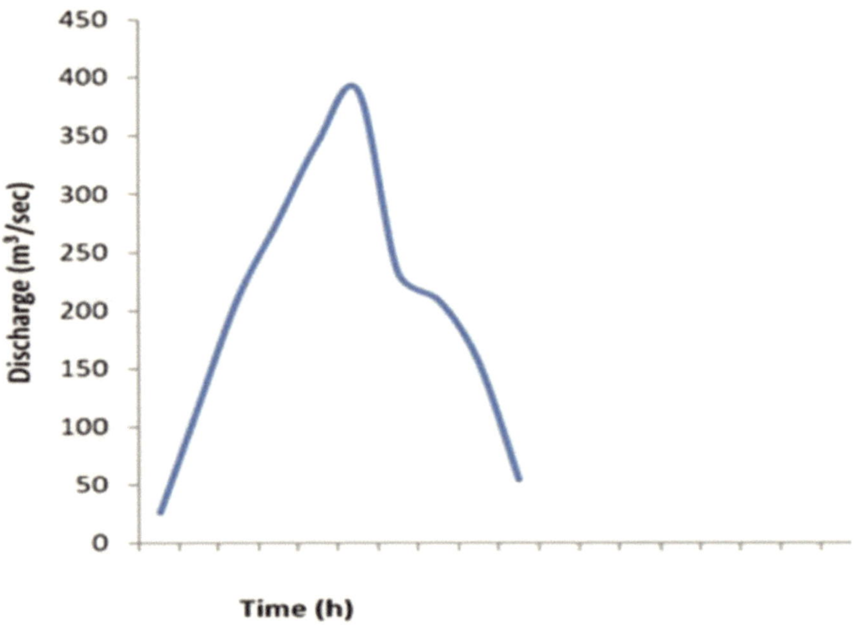

Figure 4. The synthetic unit hydrograph (UH).

The final step is the reduction of each volume to time, which is actually the calculation of the discharge. By plotting these values of discharges against time the synthetic UH is constructed. This synthetic UH is presenting on **Figure 4**. This UH reveals two vital values of the flood hydrographs which are the critical time and the maximum (peak) value of the discharge. For this empirical paradigm, these values are T_c = 18 h and the Q_{peak} = 388.667 m^3/s.

3.4. Conclusions

This methodology attempts to analyze the physical processes of a rainfall event in a hypothetical study area. Thus, a rainfall-runoff model is used for estimating the spatially distributed synthetic UH for the outlet of the catchment.

The form of the model-derived synthetic UH for the outlet of the basin can be used in a variety of cases. There are two crucial values derived from a UH, the critical time (time difference between peak rainfall and maximum discharge) and the peak value of the discharge. The development of such hydrographs can be used for extreme rainfall magnitudes in order to design constructions such as bridges and roads.

Also, UH can be used in order to extrapolate flood flow records based on rainfall records and for the development of flood forecasting and warning systems. Additionally, each UH shows the response of the catchment-study area, i.e., they provide also evaluations of extreme discharges while they are giving the opportunity to design UH (in rivers and streams) with lack of meteorological and hydrometric stations (by applying modeling on rainfall and hydrological data using GIS).

The empirical modeling described earlier has also some limitations. It undertakes uniform distribution of rainfall over the catchment and uniform intensity during the duration of rainfall excess (in case of rainfall data from rain gauge stations). In practice, these conditions are not satisfied during a real storm event. Under specific situations of nonuniform aerial scattering and disparity of intensity, UH, still, can be used if the spatial distribution is constant between different flood events. In addition, in some cases, when the rainfall data comes from meteorological stations, the catchment size levies a superior limit on the pertinency of the UH implementation due to rainfall distribution. In this case, a very big river basin needs to be tackled as the sum of smaller subcatchments. Thus, this obligation noises for an assortment of flood events of so slight a period which would generally yield a strong and approximately unchanging effective rainfall. Also it would yield a distinct single peak of hydrograph of short time base. UHs that are having the same time base are unswervingly relative to the total amount of runoff given by each hydrograph (linearity).

Usually, in hydrological modeling and especially in modeling of flash floods, there are some definite assumptions. For instance, the effects of evapotranspiration, as well as the synergy between the aquifer and the rivers, are ignored. This could also be overlooked due to the fact that the amount of evapotranspiration during the time, in which the flood occurs, is insignificant when compared to other fluxes such as infiltration. Furthermore, the effect of the aquifer-river synergy is commonly disregarded due to the response time of overland flow versus the flow within the channel. Similarly, effects of the rest of hydrological procedures such as interception and depression storage are also ignored.

3.5. Discussion

Despite the assumptions/limitations of the model, the proposed modeling provides a meaningful estimation of the maximum value of discharge and the peak time of a flood event.

The introduction of GIS technology led researchers to develop data processing automations and to produce reliable simulation models. They appreciate the standing and welfares of such a technology that empower them to evaluate data, contend with complications, generate instinctive visualization approaches, and make conclusions with a higher effectiveness.

The objective of this chapter was to present the extended history of GIS modeling and to converse the modern observes in terms of integration of GIS with the hydrological modeling, and also to discuss the problems, the assumption, and the limitations of GIS-based hydrological models. Generally, four different approaches have been widely proposed and used in terms of integrating GIS with the hydrological modeling. These are (a) embedding GIS-like functionalities into hydrological modeling software, (b) embedding hydrological modeling into GIS software, (c) loose coupling (add-on), and (d) tight coupling which actually is to customize applications into a GIS software [95].

Therefore, these models can be used as tools for policy makers in order to take decisions for the construction of artificial dams (i.e., containment barriers) and halting water projects in general. Thus, rainfall-runoff models together with the GIS technology are used as integrated systems of assessing potential impacts for various rainfall events. Hence, the GIS technology has the capability to postprocess the results which are obtaining from a model and sublimate them into policy.

Author details

Christos Chalkias[1], Nikolaos Stathopoulos[1,2], Kleomenis Kalogeropoulos[1*] and Efthimios Karymbalis[1]

*Address all correspondence to: kalogeropoulos@hua.gr

1 Department of Geography, Harokopio University, Athens, Greece

2 School of Mining and Metallurgical Engineering, Sector of Geological Sciences, Laboratory of Technical Geology and Hydrogeology, National Technical University of Athens, Greece

References

[1] Nash JE & Sutcliffe JV. Mint: River flow forecasting through conceptual models Part I —a discussion of principles. *Journal of Hydrology*. 1970;10(3):282–290.

[2] O'Connell PE, Nash JE & Farrell JP. Mint: River flow forecasting through conceptual models Part II—the Brosna catchment at Ferbane. *Journal of Hydrology*. 1970;10(4):317–329.

[3] Mandeville AN, O'Connell PE, Sutcliffe JV, & Nash JE. Mint: River flow forecasting through conceptual models Part III—the ray catchment at Grendon Underwood. *Journal of Hydrology*. 1970;11(2):109–128.

[4] Beven KJ & Kirkby MJ. Mint: Physically based, variable contributing area model of basin hydrology. *Hydrological Sciences Bulletin des Sciences Hydrologiques*. 1979;24(1):43–69.

[5] Rodríguez-Iturbe I, Valdés JB. Mint: The geomorphologic structure of hydrologic response. *Water Resources Research*. 1979:15(6):1409–1420.

[6] Kitanidis PK & Bras RL. Mint: Real-time forecasting with a conceptual hydrologic model: 2 applications and results. *Water Resources Research*. 1980;16(6):1034–1044.

[7] Kitanidis PK & Bras RL. Mint: Real-time forecasting with a conceptual hydrologic model: 1 analysis of uncertainty. *Water Resources Research*. 1980;16(6):1025–1033.

[8] O'Callaghan JF & Mark DM. Mint: The extraction of drainage networks from digital elevation data. *Computer Vision, Graphics, and Image Processing*. 1984;28(3):323–344.

[9] Hutchinson MF. Mint: A new procedure for gridding elevation and stream line data with automatic removal of spurious pits. *Journal of Hydrology*. 1989;106(3-4):211–232.

[10] Abbott MB, Bathurst JC, Cunge JA, O'Connell PE & Rasmussen J. Mint: An introduction to the European Hydrological system — Systeme Hydrologique Europeen, "SHE," 1: History and philosophy of a physically based, distributed modelling system. *Journal of Hydrology*. 1986;87(1–2):45–59.

[11] Abbott MB, Bathurst JC, Cunge JA, O'Connell PE & Rasmussen J. Mint: An introduction to the European Hydrological system—Systeme Hydrologique Europeen, "SHE", 2: Structure of a physically based, distributed modelling system. *Journal of Hydrology*, 1986;87(1–2):61–77.

[12] Beven K. Mint: Changing ideas in hydrology—The case of physically based models. *Journal of Hydrology*. 1989;105(1–2):157–172.

[13] Maidment DR. Developing a spatially distributed unit hydrograph by using GIS applications of geographic information systems in hydrology and water resources management. In: *Proceedings of EGU International Conference*; 1993; Vienna: pp. 181–192.

[14] Daly C, Neilson RP & Phillips, DL. Mint: A statistical—topographic model for mapping climatological precipitation over mountainous terrain. *Journal of Applied Meteorology*. 1994;33(2):140–158.

[15] Montgomery DR & Dietrich WE. Mint: A physically based model for the topographic control on shallow landsliding. *Water Resources Research*. 1994;30(4):1153–1171.

[16] Zhang W & Montgomery DR. Mint: Digital elevation model grid size, landscape representation, and hydrologic simulations. *Water Resources Research*. 1994;30(4):1019–1028.

[17] Wigmosta MS, Vail LW, & Lettenmaier DP. Mint: A distributed hydrology—vegetation model for complex terrain. *Water Resources Research*. 1994;30(6):1665–1679.

[18] Sellers PJ, Randall DA, Collatz GJ, Collelo GD, & Bounoua L. Mint: a revised land surface parameterization (SiB2) for atmospheric GCMs. Part I: Model formulation. *Journal of Climate*. 1996;9(4):676–705.

[19] Sellers PJ, Compton JT, Collatz GJ, Los SO, Justice CO, Dazlich DA, & Randall DA. Mint: A revised land surface parameterization (SiB2) for atmospheric GCMs. Part II: the generation of global fields of terrestrial biophysical parameters from satellite data. *Journal of Climate*. 1996;9(4):706–737.

[20] Morgan RPC, Quinton JN, Smith RE, Torri D, & Styczen ME. Mint: The European soil erosion model (EUROSEM): a dynamic approach for predicting sediment transport from fields and small catchments. *Earth Surface Processes and Landforms*. 1998;23(6):527–544.

[21] Muzik I. Mint: flood modelling with GIS-derived distributed unit hydrographs. *Hydrological Processes*. 1996;10(10):1401–1409.

[22] Iverson RM. Mint: landslide triggering by rain infiltration. *Water Resources Research*. 2000;36(7):1897–1910.

[23] Vörösmarty CJ, Green P, Salisbury J, & Lammers RB. Mint: Global water resources: vulnerability from climate change and population growth. *Science*. 2000;289(5477):284–288.

[24] Houser PR, Shuttleworth W Famiglietti JS, Gupta HV, Syed KH, & Goodrich DC. Mint: integration of soil moisture remote sensing and hydrologic modeling using data assimilation. *Water Resources Research*. 1998;34(12):3405–3420.

[25] Jackson TJ, Le Vine DM, Hsu AY, Oldak A, Starks PJ, Swift CT, Isham JD, & Haken M. Mint: Soil moisture mapping at regional scales using microwave radiometry: the Southern great plains hydrology experiment IEEE. *Transactions on Geoscience and Remote Sensing*. 1999;37(5):2136–2151.

[26] Dawson CW & Wilby R. Mint: An artificial neural network approach to rainfall-runoff modeling. *Hydrological Sciences Journal*. 1998;43(1):47–66.

[27] Dawson CW & Wilby R. Mint: Hydrological modeling using artificial neural networks. *Progress in Physical Geography*. 2001;25(1):80–108.

[28] Govindaraju RS. Mint: Artificial neural networks in hydrology I: Preliminary concepts. *Journal of Hydrologic Engineering*. 2000;5(2):115–123.

[29] Govindaraju RS. Mint: Artificial neural networks in hydrology II: Hydrologic applications. *Journal of Hydrologic Engineering*. 2000;5(2):124–137.

[30] Tarboton DG, Bras RL, & Rodriguez-Iturbe I. Mint: On the extraction of channel networks from digital elevation data. *Hydrological Processes*. 1991;5(1):81–100.

[31] Moore ID, Grayson RB, & Ladson AR. Mint: Digital terrain modelling: a review of hydrological, geomorphological, and biological applications. *Hydrological Processes*. 1991;5(1):3–30.

[32] Quinn P, Beven K, Chevallier P, & Planchon O. Mint: Prediction of hillslope flow paths for distributed hydrological modelling using digital terrain models. *Hydrological Processes*. 1991;5(1):59–79.

[33] Fairfield J & Leymarie P. Mint: Drainage networks from grid digital elevation models. *Water Resources Research*. 1991;27(5):709–717.

[34] Tarboton DG. Mint: A new method for the determination of flow directions and upslope areas in grid digital elevation models. *Water Resources Research*. 1997;33(2):309–319.

[35] Bates PD, De Roo, & APJ. Mint: A simple raster-based model for flood inundation simulation. *Journal of Hydrology*. 2000;236(1–2):54–77.

[36] Beven K. Mint: How far can we go in distributed hydrological modelling? *Hydrology and Earth System Sciences*. 2001;5(1):1–12.

[37] Thiemann M, Trosset M, Gupta H, & Sorooshian S. Mint: Bayesian recursive parameter estimation for hydrologic models. *Water Resources Research*. 2001;37(10): 2521–2535.

[38] Ajami NK, Duan Q, & Sorooshian S. Mint: An integrated hydrologic Bayesian multimodel combination framework: confronting input, parameter, and model structural uncertainty in hydrologic prediction. *Water Resources Research*. 2007;43(1):W01403.

[39] Hock R. Mint: Temperature index melt modelling in mountain areas. *Journal of Hydrology*. 2003;282(1–4):104–115.

[40] Döll P, Kaspar F, & Lehner B. Mint: A global hydrological model for deriving water availability indicators: model tuning and validation. *Journal of Hydrology*. 2003;270(1–2):105–134.

[41] Alcamo J, Döll P, Henrichs T, Kaspar F, Lehner B, Rösch T, & Siebert S. Mint: Development and testing of the WaterGAP 2 global model of water use and availability. *Hydrological Sciences Journal*. 2003;48(3):317–338.

[42] Nayak PC, Sudheer KP, Rangan DM, & Ramasastri KS. Mint: A neuro-fuzzy computing technique for modeling hydrological time series. *Journal of Hydrology*. 2004; 291(1–2): 52–66.

[43] Smith MB, Seo DJ, Koren VI, Reed SM, Zhang Z, Duan Q, Moreda F, Cong S. Mint: The distributed model intercomparison project (DMIP): motivation and experiment design. *Journal of Hydrology*. 2004;298(1–4):4–26.

[44] Arnold JG & Fohrer N. Mint: SWAT2000: Current capabilities and research opportunities in applied watershed modeling. *Hydrological Processes*. 2005;19(3):563–572.

[45] Abbaspour KC, Yang J, Maximov I, Siber R, Bogner K, Mieleitner J, Zobrist J, & Srinivasan R. Mint: Modelling hydrology and water quality in the pre-alpine/alpine Thur watershed using SWAT. *Journal of Hydrology*. 2007;333(2–4):413–430.

[46] Kalogeropoulos K, Chalkias C, Pissias E, & Karalis S. Application of the SWAT model for the investigation of reservoirs creation. In: Lambrakis N et al., editors. *Advances in the Research of Aquatic Environment*. New York: Springer-Verlag, Berlin, Heidelberg; 2011. Vol. II: pp.71–79.

[47] Kalogeropoulos K & Chalkias C. Mint: Modelling the impacts of climate change on surface runoff in small Mediterranean catchments: empirical evidence from Greece. *Water and Environment Journal*. 2013;27(4):505–513.

[48] Rienecker MM, Suarez MJ, Gelaro R, (...), Sienkiewicz M, & Woollen J. Mint: MERRA: NASA's modern-era retrospective analysis for research and applications. *Journal of Climate*. 2011;24(14):3624–3648.

[49] Weng Q. Mint: Modeling urban growth effects on surface runoff with the integration of remote sensing and GIS. *Environmental Management*. 2001;28(6):737–748.

[50] Fortin J, Turcotte R, Massicotte S, Moussa R, Fitzback J & Villeneuve J. Mint: Distributed watershed model compatible with remote sensing and GIS data I: description of model. *Journal of Hydrologic Engineering*. 2001;6(2):91–99.

[51] Di Luzio M, Srinivasan R, & Arnold JG. Mint: Integration of watershed tools and SWAT model into BASINS. *Journal of the American Water Resources Association*. 2002;38(4):1127–1141.

[52] Miller SN, Kepner WG, Mehaffey MH, Hernadez M, Miller RC, Goodrich DC, Devonald KK, Heggem DT, & Miller WP. Mint: Integrating landscape assessment and hydrologic modeling for land cover change analysis. *Journal of the American Water Resources Association*. 2002;38(4):915–929.

[53] Liu YB, Gebremeskel S, De Smedt F, Hoffmann L, & Pfister L. Mint: A diffusive transport approach for flow routing in GIS-based flood modeling. *Journal of Hydrology*. 2003;283(1-4):91–106.

http://dx.doi.org/10.5772/62824

[54] Al-Sabhan W, Mulligan M, & Blackburn GA. Mint: A real-time hydrological model for flood prediction using GIS and the WWW Computers. *Environment and Urban Systems*. 2003;27(1):9–32.

[55] Huggel C, Kääb A, Haeberli W, & Krummenacher B. Mint: Regional-scale GIS-models for assessment of hazards from glacier lake outbursts: evaluation and application in the Swiss Alps. *Natural Hazards and Earth System Science*. 2003;3(6):647–662.

[56] Lan HX, Zhou CH, Wang LJ, Zhang HY, & Li RH. Mint: Landslide hazard spatial analysis and prediction using GIS in the Xiaojiang watershed, Yunnan, China. *Engineering Geology*. 2004;76(1–2):109–128.

[57] Jain MK, Kothyari UC, & Ranga Raju KG. Mint: A GIS based distributed rainfall-runoff model. *Journal of Hydrology*. 2004;299(1–2):107–135.

[58] Knebl MR, Yang ZL, Hutchison K, & Maidment DR. Mint: Regional scale flood modeling using NEXRAD rainfall, GIS, and HEC-HMS/ RAS: A case study for the San Antonio River Basin Summer 2002 storm event. *Journal of Environmental Management*. 2005;75(4):325–336.

[59] Kyoung JL, Engel BA, Tang Z, Choi J, Ki-Sung K, Muthukrishnan S, & Tripathy D. Mint: Automated web GIS based hydrograph analysis tool, WHAT. *Journal of the American Water Resources Association*. 2005;41(6):1407–1416.

[60] Jia Y, Wang H, Zhou Z, Qiu Y, Luo X, Wang J, Yan D, & Qin D. Mint: Development of the WEP-L distributed hydrological model and dynamic assessment of water resources in the Yellow River basin. *Journal of Hydrology*. 2006;331(3–4):606–629.

[61] Olivera F, Valenzuela M, Srinivasan R, Choi J, Cho H, Koka S, & Agrawal A. Mint: ArcGIS-SWAT: A geodata model and GIS interface for SWAT. *Journal of the American Water Resources Association*. 2006;42(2):295–309.

[62] Wolski P, Savenije HHG, Murray-Hudson M, & Gumbricht T. Mint: Modelling of the flooding in the Okavango Delta, Botswana, using a hybrid reservoir-GIS model. *Journal of Hydrology*. 2006;331(1–2):58–72.

[63] Melesse AM & Graham WD. Mint: Storm runoff prediction based on a spatially distributed travel time method utilizing remote sensing and GIS. *Journal of the American Water Resources Association*. 2004;40(4):863–879.

[64] Pandey A, Chowdary VM, & Mal BC. Mint: Identification of critical erosion prone areas in the small agricultural watershed using USLE, GIS and remote sensing. *Water Resources Management*. 2007;21(4):729–746.

[65] Miller SN, Semmens DJ, Goodrich DC, Hernandez M, Miller RC, Kepner WG, & Guertin DP. Mint: The automated geospatial watershed assessment tool. *Environmental Modelling and Software*. 2007;22(3):365–377.

[66] Rahman A. Mint: A GIS based DRASTIC model for assessing groundwater vulnerability in shallow aquifer in Aligarh, India. *Applied Geography*. 2008;28(1):32–53.

[67] Jonkman SN, Bočkarjova M, Kok M, & Bernardini P. Mint: Integrated hydrodynamic and economic modelling of flood damage in the Netherlands. *Ecological Economics*. 2008;66(1):77–90.

[68] Maksimović Č, Prodanović D, Boonya-Aroonnet S, Leitao JP, Djordjević S, & Allitt R. Mint: Overland flow and pathway analysis for modelling of urban pluvial flooding. *Journal of Hydraulic Research*. 2009;47(4):512–523.

[69] Chen J, Hill AA, & Urbano LD. Mint: A GIS-based model for urban flood inundation. *Journal of Hydrology*. 2009;373(1–2):184–192.

[70] Milewski A, Sultan M, Yan E, Becker R, Abdeldayem A, Soliman F, & Gelil KA. Mint: A remote sensing solution for estimating runoff and recharge in arid environments. *Journal of Hydrology*. 2009;373(1–2):1–14.

[71] Sheikh V, Visser S, & Stroosnijder L. Mint: A simple model to predict soil moisture: bridging event and continuous hydrological (BEACH) modelling. *Environmental Modelling and Software*. 2009;24(4):542–556.

[72] Du J, Xie H, Hu Y, Xu Y, & Xu CY. Mint: Development and testing of a new storm runoff routing approach based on time variant spatially distributed travel time method. *Journal of Hydrology*. 2009;369(1–2):44–54.

[73] Chow V, Maidment D, & Mays L. *Applied Hydrology*. McGraw-Hill Education; 1988.

[74] Van der Knijff JM, Younis J, & De Roo APJ. Mint: LISFLOOD: A GIS-based distributed model for river basin scale water balance and flood simulation. *International Journal of Geographical Information Science*. 2010;24(2):189–212.

[75] Rozalis S, Morin E, Yair Y, & Price C. Mint: Flash flood prediction using an uncalibrated hydrological model and radar rainfall data in a Mediterranean watershed under changing hydrological conditions. *Journal of Hydrology*. 2010;394(1–2):245–255.

[76] Kourgialas NN, Karatzas GP, & Nikolaidis NP. Mint: An integrated framework for the hydrologic simulation of a complex geomorphological river basin. *Journal of Hydrology*. 2010;381(3–4):308–321.

[77] Paiva RCD, Collischonn W, & Tucci CEM. Mint: Large scale hydrologic and hydrodynamic modeling using limited data and a GIS based approach. *Journal of Hydrology*. 2011; 406(3–4):170–181.

[78] Lei X, Wang Y, Liao W, Jiang Y, Tian Y, & Wang H. Mint: Development of efficient and cost-effective distributed hydrological modeling tool MWEasyDHM based on open-source MapWindow GIS. *Computers and Geosciences*. 2011;37(9):1476–1489.

[79] Fugura AA, Billa L, Pradhan B, Mohamed TA, & Rawashdeh S. Mint: Coupling of hydrodynamic modeling and aerial photogrammetry-derived digital surface model for

flood simulation scenarios using GIS: Kuala Lumpur flood, Malaysia. *Disaster Advances*. 2011;4(4):20–28.

[80] Kia MB, Pirasteh S, Pradhan B, Mahmud AR, Sulaiman WNA, & Moradi A. Mint: An artificial neural network model for flood simulation using GIS: Johor River Basin, Malaysia. Environmental Earth Sciences. 2012;67(1):251–264.

[81] Sarhadi A, Soltani S, & Modarres R. Mint: Probabilistic flood inundation mapping of ungauged rivers: Linking GIS techniques and frequency analysis. *Journal of Hydrology*. 2012;458–459: 68–86.

[82] López-Vicente M, Poesen J, Navas A, & Gaspar L. Mint: Predicting runoff and sediment connectivity and soil erosion by water for different land use scenarios in the Spanish Pre-Pyrenees. *Catena*. 2013;102:62–73.

[83] Paiva RCD, Collischonn W, & Buarque DC Mint: Validation of a full hydrodynamic model for large-scale hydrologic modelling in the Amazon. *Hydrological Processes*. 2013;27(3):333–346.

[84] Tehrany MS, Pradhan B, & Jebur MN. Mint: Flood susceptibility mapping using a novel ensemble weights-of-evidence and support vector machine models in GIS. *Journal of Hydrology*. 2014;512:332–343.

[85] Formetta G, Antonello A, Franceschi S, David O, & Rigon R. Mint: Hydrological modeling with components: A GIS-based open-source framework. *Environmental Modeling and Software*. 2014;55:190–200.

[86] Chen Y, Wang B, Pollino CA, Cuddy SM, Merrin LE, & Huang C. Mint: Estimate of flood inundation and retention on wetlands using remote sensing and GIS. *Ecohydrology*. 2014;7(5):1412–1420.

[87] Mahmoud SH. Mint: Investigation of rainfall-runoff modeling for Egypt by using remote sensing and GIS integration. *Catena*. 2014;120:111–121.

[88] Fiorillo F, Pagnozzi M, & Ventafridda G. Mint: A model to simulate recharge processes of karst massifs. *Hydrological Processes*. 2015;29(10):2301–2314.

[89] Krysanova V, Hattermann F, Huang S, Hesse C, Vetter T, Liersch S, Koch H, & Kundzewicz ZW. Mint: Modeling climate and land-use change impacts with SWIM: lessons learnt from multiple applications. *Hydrological Sciences Journal*. 2015;60(4):606–635.

[90] Olivera F & Maidment D. Mint: Geographic information systems (GIS)-based spatially distributed model for runoff routing. *Polygraph International*. 1999;1:1155–1164.

[91] Kalogeropoulos K, Karalis S, Karymbalis E, Chalkias C, Chalkias G, & Katsafados P. Modeling flash floods in Vouraikos River mouth. In: *Proceedings of the MEDCOAST Conference 2013*; Marmaris, Turkey; 2013. Vol. II: pp. 1135–1146.

[92] Chow VT. *Open-Channel Hydraulics*. New York, McGraw-Hill; 1959.

[93] Hutchinson MF. ANUDEM. Version 463. Canberra: Australian National University, Centre for Environmental Studies; 2003.

[94] Callow JN & Van Niel KP, Boggs GS. Mint: How does modifying a DEM to reflect known hydrology affect subsequent terrain analysis? *Journal of Hydrology*. 2007;332(1–2):30–39.

[95] Sui DZ & Maggio RC. Integrating GIS with hydrologic modeling: practices, problems and prospects. *Computers, Environment and Urban Systems* 1999;23:33–51.

Chapter 5

Critical Loss Analyses in Korean Liquor Mergers

Jeon Seonghoon

Additional information is available at the end of the chapter

http://dx.doi.org/10.5772/63225

Abstract

The SSNIP(Small but Significant Nontransitory Increase in Price) test is a well-known conceptual framework of market definition for competition policies in most countries. Critical loss analysis is a practical method that implements the principle of SSNIP test in a quantitative way to determine whether the relevant market for an antitrust case should be enlarged or not. The method and empirical results have been successfully adopted in defining markets relevant to Korean merger cases in soju and beer industries (Moohak-Daesun in 2002 and Hite-Jinro in 2005), providing useful references for the Korean Court and Fair Trade Commission. This paper introduces the actual applications of critical loss analyses in these cases and remarks on several issues brought in the course of applications.

Keywords: merger, market definition, SSNIP, critical loss, Korean liquor industry

1. Introduction

The SSNIP test is a well-known conceptual framework of market definition for the purpose of competition policies in most countries. Critical loss analysis is a practical method which implements the principle of SSNIP test in a quantitative way to determine whether the relevant market for an antitrust case should be enlarged or not. The method has been referred to in many antitrust court cases as well as US and UK competition authorities' guidelines of market definition. Critical loss analysis is now popular among experts on competition policies in Korea since it has been successfully adopted in economics analyses of recent two merger cases in soju and beer industries.[1]

[1] Soju is popular liquor in Korea which is a kind of spirit with alcoholic content of about 20–22%. There are two kinds of soju—distilled and diluted. Popular one in Korea is the diluted, which are made by diluting alcohol essence extracted from grains—ethanol made from rice, barley, corn, etc. The sales of diluted soju in 2004 were about 2.34 trillion won. Total liquor sales were 6.64 trillion won in 2004. Hence, diluted soju accounts for 35.2% of total liquor markets. On the other hand, beer whose sales were 3.45 trillion won in 2004 accounts for 52%.

The first case is a horizontal merger between two local soju producers in 2002; Moohak, a dominant producer in Kyungnam province, attempted a hostile takeover of Daesun, a dominant producer in adjacent Busan area, through gathering shares.[2] The two producers were dominant in each region and almost close to monopolistic position with market shares more than 80%. If the geographic market was defined as the whole country, they were just fringe firms with national market shares less than 10%, while Jinro was a dominant producer with national market share more than 50%. Hence, geographic market definition is critical in evaluating anticompetitive effects of the attempted merger. Defining the relevant markets as the two regions, Korea Fair Trade Commission (KFTC afterward) made an injunctive order of shares disposal in 2003. The defendant, Moohak, appealed to the second court against the KFTC decision. Jeon submitted an economic analysis which implemented critical loss analysis using a consumption survey data.[3] The result confirmed the KFTC's market definition. The case is regarded as a landmark in antitrust enforcement in Korea in that it was the first case where economic analyses were critically important in the court decision making. That is, two parties submitted their own economic analyses on the relevant geographic market. Seoul High Court, evaluating the confronting economic analyses, made a final decision upholding the KFTC's decision in 2004.

The second case is Hite-Jinro merger in 2005; Hite and Jinro were dominant companies in the Korean beer and soju market, respectively—each with market share more than 50%. The case attracted much public attention since the merger deal amounted to 3.41 trillion won, which was unprecedented at the time. Moreover, competing companies in both beer and soju markets strongly opposed to the merger, alleging its anticompetitive effects. Their arguments were twofold. First, the demand-side substitutability between beer and soju is so high that they constitute a single product market relevant to antitrust merger evaluation, called "pub alcoholic drink." If that is the case, anticompetitive effects are out of question. Second, regardless of the definition of the relevant product market, concerns may still remain due to leverage or portfolio effects; i.e., it was alleged that the combined company could take advantage of dominance in one product market and exclude competitors in another market by using unfair methods such as exclusive tying or predatory bundling. Also, Hite-Jinro merger included a horizontal merger since Hite had a subsidiary local soju producer in Chonbuk. The anticompetitiveness of the horizontal merger depended upon the relevant geographic range of soju market. Jeon et al. submitted to KFTC economic analyses on the relevant market definitions and the possibility of anticompetitive effects.[4] We applied basically the same method of market definition as that of the previous Moohak-Daesun merger case. KFTC, concurring to most of our analyses as far as market definitions were concerned, concluded that beer and soju markets were separate product markets and that the geographic market relevant to the horizontal soju merger was basically country wide. Accordingly, KFTC approved the merger with some transitory corrective remedies attached.

---

[2] Administrative districts of South Korea are a capital city, six broad cities, and nine provinces. Busan and Kyungnam are a broad city and a province, respectively, and both southeastern.

[3] The main results of the analysis were introduced in [1]. Section 3 in this paper was based on it.

[4] The main results of the analysis were introduced in [2]. Section 4 in this paper was based on it.

http://dx.doi.org/10.5772/63225

The following section discusses the SSNIP test as a well-known principle of market definition for competition policies and explains critical loss analysis that implements the SSNIP test practically. In Sections 3 and 4, actual applications of critical loss analyses in the Moohak-Daesun and Hite-Jinro cases are introduced. The author was involved with the two cases as a principal economic expert and submitted the relevant economic reports to the court in the first case and KFTC in the second case. The court and KFTC agreed upon the author's arguments. The two sections in the paper are based on the author's analyses and the court and KFTC's judgments on the two cases. The last section concludes by remarking on several issues brought on in the course of the applications.

2. SSNIP test and critical loss analysis

Article 2.8 of the Korea Monopoly Regulation and Fair Trade Act (KMRFTA) defines the relevant market as "the range of transactions where there exist or may exist competitive relations in terms of objects, stages, or regions of trade," and KFTC merger guideline articulates it as "the set of products or the whole geographic area into which a representative consumer can switch his/her purchases in response to the small but significant and nontransitory increase in prices of the specific products or regions holding other prices constant."

The spirit is the same with SSNIP test on which antitrust enforcement agencies in the USA, EU, and many other countries base their market definition.[5] According to the US horizontal merger guideline in [4], a market is defined as "a product or a group of products and a geographic area in which it is produced or sold, such that a hypothetical profit maximizing firm, not subject to price regulation, that was the only present or future producer or seller of those products in that area likely would impose a small but significant and nontransitory increase in price, assuming the terms of sale of all other products are held constant." EU guideline in [5] specifies the question to be answered as "whether the parties' customers would switch to readily available substitutes or to suppliers located elsewhere in response to a hypothetical small (in the range 5–10%), permanent relative price increase in the products and areas being considered. If substitution would be enough to make the price increase unprofitable because of the resulting loss of sales, additional substitutes and areas are included in the relevant market. This would be done until the set of products and geographic areas is such that small, permanent increases in relative prices would be profitable."

There exists a subtle difference between market definition in Korea and that in USA. In the former, a market is defined in a consumer's perspective as the largest range where he/she can switch his/her purchases in response to SSNIP ("a representative consumer version"). In the latter, it is defined in a producer's perspective as the smallest range where he/she can make profits by SSNIP ("a hypothetical monopolist version"). The representative consumer version may imply a smaller market than the hypothetical monopolist version. The reason is as follows. The representative consumer version considers only substitution effect and includes products

[5] For SSNIP test in the historical context, see [3].

or regions which are close substitutes in the relevant market. On the other hand, the hypothetical monopolist version considers price effect, i.e., both substitution and income effects. Even if all close substitutes are included, a hypothetical monopolist may not be able to increase price profitably because of the negative income effect in case of normal goods. Hence, the range of the relevant market should be enlarged further under the hypothetical monopolist version. [6] However, it seems that the hypothetical monopolist version is more appropriate from anti-monopoly perspective, since we are concerned about the price increase regardless of its sources. Another advantage of the monopolist version is its practicality; the definition implies the critical level of sales loss that can be compared with actual sales loss after a price increase, which is the idea of critical loss analysis.

While SSNIP test is a conceptual framework of market definition for competition policies, critical loss analysis is a practical method of implementing it in real cases. The analytical method, since it was first introduced by [6], has been tried in many US antitrust cases.[7] Among enforcement agencies, UK OFT and US DOJ and FTC mention explicitly the method as a useful tool in their market definition guidelines. In Korea, Jeon introduced critical loss analysis first in an economic analysis of the geographic market definition relevant to Moohak-Daesun merger (see [1]). Seoul High Court in 2004 (case number 2003nu2252) endorsed it as "an effective and appropriate method for defining the relevant geographic market as economic analysis which applies 'SSNIP' method systematically into practical cases." Consequently, Jeon et al. applied the method again in market definitions relevant to Hite-Jinro merger, and KFTC in 2006 (decision number 2006-009) concurred with them.

The idea of critical loss analysis is simple. Profitability of a price increase depends on the amount of consequent sales loss. "Critical loss for *X*-% price increase" is defined as the maximum percentage loss of sales volume that would not result in profit loss for *X*-% price increase. To put it another way, critical loss is the minimum percentage loss of sales volume that would result in profits decrease. That is, if actual sales loss is larger (smaller) than critical loss, then the price increase will lead to profit decrease (increase).[8]

Table 1 summarizes the method of market definition using critical loss analysis.[9]

Critical loss analysis
Actual sales loss after SSNIP <

[6] I presume here normal goods with negative income effect. Discussions must be reversed in case of inferior goods.

[7] There are many examples of its applications, such as FTC v. Tenet Health Care [186 F.2d 1045 (8th Cir, 1999)], USA v. Mercy Health Services [902 F.Supp.968 (N.D. Iowa 1995)], California v. Sutter Health System [130 F. Supp. 2d 1109 (N.D. Cal. 2001)], USA v. SunGuard Data Sys., Inc. [172 F. Supp. 2nd 172 n.21 (D.D.C. 2001)], and FTC v. Swedish Match [131 F.Supp. 2nd 151 (D.D.C. 2000)]. Especially in Swedish match, both enforcement agencies and defendants tried to define the relevant market based on their own critical loss analyses, and the court, reviewing them, suggested its own interpretations. See [7].

[8] Notice that I adopt a breakeven version of critical loss rather than a profit-maximization version. The former is more often used in practices because of its simplicity and independence of the shape of demand curve.

[9] If we reinterpret sales loss due to price change as price elasticity of demand, critical loss analysis becomes critical elasticity analysis.

http://dx.doi.org/10.5772/63225

Critical loss analysis
Critical sales loss for SSNIP
⇒ Profitability of SSNIP by a hypothetical monopolist
No further market expansion

Table 1. Framework of critical loss analysis.

If actual sales loss after a SSNIP is less than critical loss corresponding to the SSNIP, then a hypothetical monopolist can make more profits by such a SSNIP, which implies that the relevant market should be confined there with no need of further expansion. It is because there are no closely substitutable products or regions to which consumers can switch their current purchases in response to a SSNIP. On the other hand, if actual sales loss after a SSNIP is more than the critical loss, then a hypothetical monopolist cannot make more profits by such a SSNIP. This implies that the relevant market should be expanded to include next available substitutes. Market definition according to critical loss analysis starts from considering a set of products and regions for which anticompetitive concerns are raised. Compare actual sales loss with critical loss repetitively until there is no need for further expansion where actual loss is less than critical loss. That is, the relevant market is the smallest market for which a hypothetical monopolist can make more profits by a SSNIP.

Denoting critical loss by *CL*, we have a very simple relationship of such dependence as follows: $CL = (X/(X + M))$.[10] Critical loss corresponding to *X*-% price increase depends on *X*. The larger a price increase is, the greater sales loss a hypothetical monopolist can endure without incurring profits loss. Another important determinant price-cost margin, $M = ((P - C)/P)$ where *P* is unit price and *C* is marginal or incremental cost. For a high rate of margins, each sale lost entails a relatively large loss of profit. Hence, a high rate of margins implies a small level of critical loss.[11]

3. Geographic market definition in Moohak-Daesun merger

3.1. Brief introduction of Moohak-Daesun case

In January 2003 the KFTC made an order that Moohak dispose all stocks of Daesun it purchased in 2002,[12] since the acquisition would restrain competition seriously in local soju markets of Busan and Kyungnam regions and infringe Article 7.1 of KMRFT Act. Daesun, the acquired one, commanded monopolistic position in Busan area with 84.4% market share in 2001, while Jinro, the largest soju producer in the country, had only 7.2% share in the region. On the other

[10] For the derivation, see [8].

[11] In interpreting the implication of a high rate of margins, we should be careful of the well-known cellophane fallacy. That is, if high current margins are due to monopoly power or collusion, a simple conversion of critical loss may mislead to an enlarged market definition. Then the starting price in calculating margins should be adjusted to a counterfactual competitive price.

[12] Moohak and its owner purchased Daesun's stocks by 41.21% from June 2002 to December 2002. See KFTC Decision 2003-027.

hand, the acquirer, Moohak, was in a monopolistic position in Kyungnam area with 84.3% market share in 2001, while other producers' market shares were insignificant except Daesun's 12.9% share in the region.

The KFTC defined the geographic market relevant to Moohak-Daesun merger as diluted soju in Busan and Kyungnam.[13] Given this market definition, the combined company achieves 91.5% share in Busan and 97.2% share in Kyungnam, and the merger meets the conditions for presumption of competitive concerns in Article 7.4.1 of KMRFT. Moreover, according to KFTC, there exist de facto entry restrictions, although not de jure ones, in the soju industry; it takes long time and enormous costs in building up brand recognition in soju market. In addition, soju producers are not allowed to engage in wholesaling. Hence, new entrants have difficulties in establishing distribution channels, since incumbent distributors already maintain long-term relationships with Moohak and Daesun in the areas.[14] Moohak appealed against the KFTC decision to Seoul High Court. But the second court reaffirmed it. The case is now regarded as a landmark in antitrust enforcement in Korea in that two parties submitted economic analyses which supported their own views on the relevant geographic market, and the court resorted to economic analyses in reaching the decision (see [1]).

In order to address Moohak-Daesun case properly, we should understand the consumers' strong loyalty to their local products in Busan and Kyungnam. Daesun in Busan gained market share by more than 20% in 1997, while Jinro, which is a nationally dominant producer, lost market share by almost 20%. Daesun strengthened its market dominance afterward and maintained around 85% share in 2000s.

	1996	1997	1998	1999	2000	2001	2002	2003
Daesun	53.5	73.9	79.8	81.5	83.9	85.0	85.7	86.9
Moohak	2.8	5.1	7.2	7.9	7.9	7.1	6.5	6.6
Jinro	37.3	18.0	9.7	7.4	6.7	6.6	6.7	5.2

Source: Korean Liquor Manufacturers Association.

Table 2. Trend of market shares in Busan (sales, %).

The situation in the Kyungnam region was similar. Moohak gained market share by more than 10% since 1998, while Jinro lost share by the corresponding amount. Moohak have maintained a strong market position afterwards, even though Daesun shaded its market share a little bit recently.

[13] The product market is confined to "diluted" soju, but not distilled one. Diluted soju is produced by some process of diluting ethanol made from grains such as rice, barley, and corn.

[14] Other defenses of efficiency and failing firm were not relevant in this case.

http://dx.doi.org/10.5772/63225

	1996	1997	1998	1999	2000	2001	2002	2003
Moohak	68.2	68.9	81.1	84.0	85.3	83.5	82.1	81.8
Daesun	8.1	10.2	9.7	10.9	10.7	13.0	13.9	14.2
Jinro	21.7	20.3	9.1	5.1	4.0	3.4	4.0	4.0

Source: Korean Liquor Manufacturers Association.

Table 3. Trend of market shares in Kyungnam (sales, %).

To understand the persistent dominance of local products and the huge shifts of market shares in these as shown in **Tables 2** and **3**, we should consider the history of regulation in local soju markets and the political power shift among regions in Korea. A regulation of mandatory purchase of local products more than 50% onto wholesalers had been introduced in order to protect local soju producers since mid-1970s. The regulation was abolished in 1992 and revived in June 1996 and finally declared illegal in December 1996 by the constitutional court. Interestingly, local characteristic has strengthened after the final abolishment of mandatory purchase of local products. First of all, local producers, confronted with more competitive pressures since mid-1990s, made greater survival efforts. Especially Daesun initiated such efforts by lowering prices and introducing new products with less alcoholic contents.[15] Moreover, the regionalism in Busan and Kyungnam became stronger after the shift of political power from their regions to another.[16] It seems that people in these regions became more cohesive in their regional compassion, and such political atmosphere strengthened the consumers' loyalty to local soju products.[17]

Generally the small but significant price increase in SSNIP test is in the range of 5–10%. But when there are a large number of consumers who are loyal to a given product, we may have to consider higher price increases as well. To be more precise, consider the following numerical example. There are 100 consumers in a region who have unit demands for a product. The current price for the product is $100, and the cost is $70. All consumers are now using the product. There are two groups of consumers: 30 price-sensitive consumers who will switch to another substitutable product if the price increases by 5% and 70 loyal consumers who stick to the product unless the price increases by more than 20%. In this situation, a hypothetical monopolist of the product cannot make more profits by a price increase of 5% or 10%:

Current profits: $3000 [=(100 − 70) × 100]

Profits after 5% price increase: $2450 [=(105 − 70) × 70]

Profits after 10% price increase: $2800 [=(110 − 70) × 70].

[15] For example, it introduced a new product of low-alcohol soju with alcohol content of 23% which was less than the contemporary standard 25% and lowered its price by 9.5% in 1996.

[16] The power base of President Park Jung Hee (1961–1978), Chun Doo Hwan (1981–87), Roh Tai Woo (1988–1992), and Kim Young Sam (1993–1997) was all Youngnam regions (Busan, Kyungnam, and Kyungbuk). On the other hand, Kim Dae Jung (1998–2002) based his power on Honam regions (Chonnam and Chonbuk).

[17] Choi et al. in [9] try to explain the persistence of market dominance in the Korean soju industry with local identity rooted in the past regulation and its strengthenment due to the change in political power configuration.

Nonetheless, the monopolist can earn more profits by a price increase of 15 or 20%:

Profits after 15% price increase: \$3150 [= (115 – 70) × 70]

Profits after 20% price increase: \$3500 [= (120 – 70) × 70].

Of course, the monopolist will increase the price by 20%. In that case, the market should be confined to the product and not be extended further. However, if we considered only 5–10% range of price increases in the SSNIP test, we might end up with extending the market by including next available substitute products or regions. Given the possibility that the hypothetical monopolist can exploit market power by a large price increase such as 20%, the danger of expanding the relevant market is serious.

3.2. Critical loss analysis

To determine whether Busan and Kyungnam are the geographic market of diluted soju relevant to Moohak-Daesun merger, we have to estimate and compare the critical and actual loss of regional sales corresponding to various levels of SSNIP.

3.2.1. Estimation of margins and critical loss

Proper margins, in an economic sense, are the difference between price and marginal cost. But average variable cost is used for marginal cost in practice because of measurement difficulties:

$$M = \frac{\text{price} - \text{marginal cost}}{\text{price}} \cong \frac{\text{price} - \text{average variable cost}}{\text{price}} \tag{1}$$

Using accounting data, the above rate of margins is measured approximately by

$$M \cong \frac{\text{sales} - \text{variable costs such as material and labor costs}}{\text{sales}} \tag{2}$$

Among various concepts of profit/loss in an income statement, operating profits are the most relevant in calculating margins. The operating profits of Moohak and Daesun in 2002 are as follows[18]:

The rate of operating profits, 27.1%, is considerably high in comparison with the food and drink industry average of 7.3% as well as the whole manufacturing industry average of 6.7%.

To convert operating profits into margins, we should deduct fixed parts from sales costs and marketing and administration costs in **Table 4**. The fixed components in sales cost are "rent" and "depreciation," and those in marketing and administration cost are "rent," "depreciation," "intangible assets deduction," "taxes and charges," "insurance," and "membership fees."

[18] We used data in 2002, the year of stock acquisition. But the results do not change materially even if we use data in 2001 or 2003.

http://dx.doi.org/10.5772/63225

Deducting these fixed costs from total costs, we can estimate the margins of Moohak and Daesun in 2002 (**Table 5**).

	Moohak	Daesun	Moohak + Daesun
Sales (A)	78,432	75,283	153,715
Sales cost (B)	42,868	38,809	81,677
Marketing and administration cost (C)	17,548	12,864	30,412
Operating profits (A – B – C)	18,016	23,610	41,625
Operating profits ratio ((A – B – C)/A)	23.0%	31.4%	27.1%

Source: Companies' annual report.

Table 4. Income statements of Moohak and Daesun in 2002 (mil. won, %).

	Moohak	Daesun	Moohak + Daesun
Sales (A)	78,432	75,283	153,715
Variable sales costs (B′)	39,996	36,616	76,612
Variable marketing and administration cost (C′)	16,173	11,870	28,043
Margins ratio ((A – B′ – C′)/A)	28.4%	35.6%	31.9%

Source: Companies' annual report.

Table 5. Margins of Moohak and Daesun in 2002 (mil. won, %).

The other party on Moohak's side commented that the estimated ratio of margins, 31.9%, was misleadingly too low. They contended that fixed components should be defined as those which do not depend on operation level in one year and accordingly regarded "wages and salaries," expenses for "training," "advertising," and "maintenance" should be regarded as fixed costs as well as "rent," "depreciation," "intangible asset deduction," "taxes and charges," "insurance," and "membership fees."[19] But Seoul High Court decision in 2004 made it clear that those costs such as labor, advertising, and maintenance are not easily regarded as fixed during the significant period over which monopoly power can be exercised (the relevant time horizon should not be confined to the period of one year).

Given $M = 31.9\%$, critical losses corresponding to various levels of SSNIP, $X = 5\%$, 10%, 15%, and 30%, are calculated by the formula of $CL = (X/(X + M))$ (**Table 6**).

[19] Including all those components as fixed, they estimated the margins as high as 47.1%. Even with such a high estimate, the actual losses are less than the critical losses for 15% and 30% increases in price, and the relevant market should be confined to local regions, for consumption in dining/drinking houses. On the other hand, the actual losses are greater than the critical losses for 5–30% increases in price, and the relevant geographic market may be enlarged, for consumption in retailing shops. Hence, the results with large fixed costs and high margins may be mixed. As a comparison, the results with our estimated margins of 31.9% imply consistently a narrow local market for all price increases above 10% as shown in **Tables 7** and **8**.

	X = 5%	X = 10%	X = 15%	X = 30%
Critical loss	13.6%	23.9%	32.0%	48.5%

Table 6. Critical losses for the estimated margins of 31.9%.

We will consider high levels of SSNIP such as 15% and 30% as well as conventional 5% and 10%. Such consideration is warranted by heterogeneous composition of consumers with loyal majority and price-sensitive minority in Busan and Kyungnam. As shown by the previous numerical example, dominant local companies may disregard price-sensitive consumers and employ a high price strategy for loyal consumers in the circumstance. The possibility of high price strategy has significant implications on geographic market definition discussed in the following.

3.2.2. Estimation of actual sales loss and geographic market definition

We used a survey data of consumers' choice of soju products in Busan and Kyungnam, estimated consumers' purchase substitution in response of price changes, and consequent actual sales loss. The sample size is 1042, and the sampling error is 3.03.[20] The number of consumers whose favorite soju was either Daesun or Moohak was 945. They were questioned whether they would switch consumption into Jinro if the price of "Dasesun's C1" or "Moohak's White" relative to the price of "Jinro's Chamiseul" increased in each of two places—"dining/drinking houses" (e.g., restaurants or pubs) and "retailing shops" (e.g., convenience stores or supermarkets). The amounts of soju consumption in two places are said to be comparable in terms of quantities. But soju prices in the former are almost three times higher than those in the latter. Also it may be the case that consumption behavior might be different in two places since people usually drink together with others in the former while buying for in-house consumption in the latter. However, it turned out that the results based on the data of the former were very similar to those on the data of the latter.

This analysis starts from an integrated region of Busan and Kyungnam, and consider whether the relevant geographic market should be enlarged further or not. If a hypothetical monopolist in Busan and Kyungnam could increase profits by an SSNIP, then the geographic expansion of the relevant market is not necessary. If that is the case, it is not necessary to consider whether the market should be separated into each of Busan and Kyungnam since anticompetitive concerns on Moohak-Daesun merger are serious enough as long as the relevant market is local, regardless of whether the relevant market is Busan and Kyungnam separate or combined.

Table 7 and **8** summarizes the results of our critical loss analyses.

---

[20] Gallup Korea conducted a survey in 2004 in Busan and parts of Kyungnam province—Yangsan, Kimhae, and Masan; Busan is Daesun's base, Yangsan adjacent to Busan is where Daesun has strength, Kimhae is a competing field of Daesun and Moohak, and Masan is Moohak's base.

	Actual loss vs. critical loss	Enlarge the geographic market beyond Busan and Kyungnam?
5% increase	14.6 > 13.6%	Yes
10% increase	19.9 < 23.9%	*No*
15% increase	23.2 < 32.0%	*No*
30% increase	34.5 < 48.5%	*No*

Table 7. Critical loss analyses with data of dining/drinking houses.

	Actual loss vs. critical loss	Enlarge the geographic market beyond Busan and Kyungnam?
5% increase	15.8 > 13.6%	Yes
10% increase	21.0 < 23.9%	*No*
15% increase	25.5 < 32.0%	*No*
30% increase	43.4 < 48.5%	*No*

Table 8. Critical loss analyses with data of retailing shops.

We obtain similar estimates of actual losses and the same results of critical loss analyses, with data of retailing shops.

The above results show that a hypothetical monopolist in Busan and Kyungnam region could not increase profits by a low SSNIP of 5%, but could do so by higher SSNIPs such as 10%, 15%, and even 30%. This is because there are two groups of consumers in the region—a large group of price-insensitive consumers who are loyal to local products and a small group of price-sensitive ones; a monopolist can opt for a high price strategy to exploit loyal consumers, taking the risk of losing price-sensitive customers. To conclude our critical loss analyses, our results indicate that the geographic market of diluted soju product relevant to Moohak-Daesun merger is confined to the local area within Busan and Kyungnam province and not extended to the country as a whole.

How sensitive are the above results to the breakdown of loyal and price-sensitive consumers? To address this question, it is helpful to interpret the critical analyses above in a reverse way. From **Tables 7** and **8**, we know that the critical percentage of "strongly" loyal consumers who would stick to local soju unless the price increase is higher than 30% is 51.5%. On the other hand, the actual percentage of such loyal consumers is 65.5% with the data of dining/drinking houses and 56.6% with the data of retailing shops. If we regard the consumers who would stick to local soju unless the price increase is higher than 10% as "broadly defined" loyal consumers, then the critical percentage of such loyal consumers is 76.1%, while the actual percentage of loyal consumers is 80.1% with the data of dining/drinking houses and 79.0% with the data of retailing shops. Hence, regardless of the criterion of loyalty, and the place of consumption, the hypothetical monopolist has the sufficient percentage of consumers to exploit their loyalty with price increases higher than 10%.

We can confirm the locality of the relevant geographic market with the complimentary analysis of LIFO-LOFI indexes.[21] LIFO defined by regional production's share in regional total consumption for a give product is 94.6%, while LOFI defined by regional consumption's share in regional production for a give product is 99.3%. A high ratio of LIFO means "Little In From the Outside," while a high ratio of LOFI means "Little Out From the Inside." It is a rule of thumb that LIFO and LOFI about as high as 75–90% are regarded as implying the establishment of regional market.

3.3. Implications for anticompetitive effects of Moohak-Daesun merger

The market definition in antitrust cases is a starting point of analyzing anticompetitive effects of mergers and consequent dominant position. The Korean competition law presumes "a combination of enterprises" as "practically suppressing competition in any particular business area" if all of the following conditions in Article 7.4 are met:

a. The combined company is in a dominant position in the relevant market; i.e., its market share is 50% or more, or CR-3 is 75% or more except that its market share is less than 10%.

b. The combined market share is the largest in the relevant market.

c. The difference between the combined market share and the next largest market share is 25% or more.

Denoting the largest, the second largest, and the third market share by s_1, s_2, and s_3, respectively, we can recapitulate the above presumptive conditions as follows: the combined market share should be s_1 and should satisfy either (i) or (ii):

$s_1 \geq 50$ %, and $s_1 \geq (4/3)s_2$

$10 \% \leq s_1 \leq 50$ %, $s_1 + s_2 + s_3 \geq 75$ %, and $s_1 \geq (4/3)s_2$

The impact of the Moohak-Daesun merger on market concentration hinges critically on the range of relevant geographic market (**Table 9**).

	Busan (BS)	Kyungnam (KN)	BS + KN	Korea
Daesun (DS)	85.7%	13.9%	50.6%	7.8%
Moohak (MH)	6.5%	82.1%	44.0%	7.5%
DS + MH	92.2%	96.0%	94.6%	15.3%
Jinro	6.7%	4.0%	5.0%	53.7%

Source: Korean Liquor Manufacturers Association.

Table 9. Market shares of Moohak-Daesun in 2002.

[21] The indexes of LIOF and LOFI were first formalized by [10]. Recently, they often have been used for geographic market definition in US hospital mergers: e.g., USA v. Rockford Memorial Hospital [717 F. Supp. 1251 (N.D. Ill. 1989)], FTC v. Freeman Hospital [911 F. Supp. 1213 (W.D. MO. 1995), FTC v. Butterworth Health Corp. [946 F. Supp. 1285 (W.D. Mich. 1996), and USA v. Long Island Jewish Medical Center [983 F. Supp. 121 (E.D.N.Y. 1997).

If the relevant market is confined to Busan, Kyungnam, or the integrated region of BS + KN, it is obvious that the merger meets the conditions of presumption on suppression of competition according to KMRFTA. In fact, the market gets close to monopoly. On the other hand, if the market is national, then the merger does not belong to even the range of concerns about possible restraint on competition according to KFTC's guideline.

4. Market definitions in Hite-Jinro merger

4.1. Brief description of related events

Hite bought 52.1% shares of Jinro's stocks in August 2005. The size of Hite was 1852 bil. won and 861 bil. won in terms of assets and sales, respectively, in 2004. Its main product was beer, and the national share in beer market was 60.2% in 2004. On the other hand, the size of Jinro was 923 bil. won and 693 bil. won in terms of assets and sales, respectively, in 2004. Its main product was soju, and the national share in soju market was 55.8% in 2004. Hite has a subsidiary soju company, Hitejujo, which had a national market share of 1.5%. Even though Hitejujo is not a significant producer in the national soju market, it has the largest market share of 50.6% in Chonbuk province where Jinro is the second largest with 42.5% in 2004.[22]

Competitive concerns about Hite-Jinro merger and problems of the relevant market definition were twofold: one for a merger between Hite beer and Jinro soju and another for a merger between Hitejujo soju and Jinro soju. For the first one, the parties opposing the merger, especially OB beer which almost halves Korean beer market with Hite, alleged that beer and soju are substitutes so close that they constitute a single product market relevant to the merger, the so-called pub alcoholic drink. If that is the case, the merger would be very difficult to go through since it would be a horizontal merger with a significant increase in concentration (**Table 10**).

	Sales (mil. won)	Share
Hite*	837,598	34.0%
Jinro	613,254	24.9%
OB**	543,313	22.1%
Others***	468,245	19.0%
Total	2,462,410	100.0%

*Hite beer + Hitejujo soju.
**OB beer + Cass beer (both brands belong to the same company).
***All others are local soju producers such as Moohak, Daesun, and Keumbokju.
Source in [11]. Sales are in terms of net sales amount before taxes.

Table 10. "Pub alcoholic drink" market in 2004.

[22] Hite and Jinro sell spring water, but the market is very competitive in that they are just two among many producers with market shares of 6.2% and 10.5%, respectively. No competitive concerns were raised in that regard.

On the other hand, if beer and soju are regarded as separate products, the merger is basically conglomerate. In that case, there still may remain some anticompetitive concerns since both beer and soju companies share the same channels of wholesale distribution. But the anticompetitive allegations will be sagging.

The second horizontal part of the merger was not a big issue since Hitejujo was a relatively small company. But an interesting issue here was whether the relevant geographic market was confined to the local province of Chonbuk or extended nationwide. Recall that the geographic soju market relevant to Moohak-Daesun merger was confined to the local areas of Busan and Kyungnam. If the geographic market was defined locally in this case too, e.g., as Chonbuk, then the horizontal merger would create a virtual monopoly in the region; the combination of Hitejujo and Jinro would have a market share of 92.8% in Chonbuk. On the other hand, if the relevant market is national, market concentration does not change consequentially.

In this case, Jeon et al. submitted to KFTC economic analyses on behalf of Hite (see [2]). They defined the relevant product market for the first conglomerate case as two separate markets of beer and soju and the relevant geographic market for the second horizontal one as the national market in soju excluding some southern regions. On the other hand, Ryu and Yi in [10] in behalf of OB Beer Company contended that the relevant product market was a single market of beer and soju, the so-called pub alcoholic drinks. Interestingly, both parties applied the same method of market definition—critical loss analysis. However, their estimates of actual and critical losses were different, which led to conflicting conclusions on the relevant product market definition.

Reviewing both parties' economic analyses, Korea Fair Trade Commission adopted the market definitions by Jeon et al. KFTC final decision in 2006 was to allow the merger with some behavioral remedies attached. The remedies included a price cap of RPI + 5% on Hite and Jinro's beer and soju, the division of marketing workforce and organization of Hite and Jinro for five years, and the provision of some arrangements by Hite itself that would ensure it not to commit exclusionary practices in the future.

4.2. Critical loss analysis for product market definition

In the following, I summarize the part of Jeon et al.'s analyses on the definition of product market relevant to Hite-Jinro merger.

4.2.1. Estimation of margins and critical loss

We can apply the same method of calculating margins of soju and beer industries as was introduced in the previous section. The rate of margins in soju industry was calculated with income and cost statements of Jinro in 2003 and 2004 (**Table 11**).

http://dx.doi.org/10.5772/63225

	Jinro (03)	Jinro (04)	Jinro (03 + 04)
Sales (A)	615,973	693,053	1,309,026
Variable sales costs (B′)	317,187	338,827	656,014
Variable market and administration costs (C′)	134,736	126,373	261,109
Margin ratio ((A − B′ − C′)/A)	26.6%	32.9%	29.9%

Source: Jinro's annual report.

Table 11. Margins of Jinro in 2003 and 2004 (mil. won, %).

Given Jinro's dominant position in soju industry, we may regard the estimated rate of margins, 29.9%, as the representative one for soju industry. Incidentally, it is not much different from 27.1% that we obtained previously for Moohak-Daesun case.

Since beer industry is a duopoly, we use the data of Hite and OB in calculating margins (**Table 12**).

	Hite (03 + 04)	OB (03 + 04)	Hite + OB (03 + 04)
Sales (A)	1,683,146	1,209,923	2,893,069
Variable sales costs (B′)	721,850	471,604	1,193,455
Variable marketing and administration costs (C′)	478,914	417,495	896,409
Margin ratio ((A − B′ − C′)/A)	28.7%	26.5%	27.8%

Source: Companies' annual report.

Table 12. Margins of Hite and Jinro in 2003 and 2004 (mil. won, %).

The estimated rate of margins for beer industry, 27.8%, is slightly lower than that for soju industry, 29.9%.

On the other hand, Ryu and Yi in [10] estimated the rates of margins for soju and beer industries as 52.6% and 53.2%, respectively. The difference comes from their classification of fixed costs and, more fundamentally, their perspective of "nontransitory" period in SSNIP. They contended that fixed components should be defined as those which are fixed regardless of operation level within the period of one year, and accordingly regarded "wages and salaries," expenses for "training," "advertising," and "maintenance" should be regarded as fixed costs as well as "rents," "depreciation," "intangible assets deduction," "taxes and charges," "insurance," and "membership fees." As noted before, Seoul High Court in regard to Moohak-Daesun case decided that those costs such as labor, advertising, and maintenance are not easily regarded as fixed during the significant period over which monopoly power can be exercised. Concurring to this decision, KFTC rebutted the high estimates of margins by Ryu and Yi; "they made an error of overestimating margins by regarding the time horizon dividing variable and fixed costs as one year rather than a significant period for exercising monopoly power, and consequently overestimating variable costs."

Given rate of margins (M) and price increase (X), critical loss (CL) is derived from $CL = (X/(X + M))$. For soju industry with $M = 29.9\%$, critical losses corresponding to $X = 5\%$ and 10% are (**Table 13**):

	$X = 5\%$	$X = 10\%$
Critical loss	14.3%	25.0%

Table 13. Critical losses for soju industry.

For beer industry with $M = 27.8\%$, they are (**Table 14**):

	$X = 5\%$	$X = 10\%$
Critical loss	15.3%	26.5%

Table 14. Critical losses for beer industry.

Notice that we considered only 5% and 10% levels of SSNIP in this case. This is because we expect that consumer loyalty is usually associated to specific brands within a product, but not to a product as a whole. That is, consumers may be loyal to some specific brand in comparison with all other brands in a product, but not loyal to a specific product in comparison with all other products. Hence we do not expect that there are a small group of price-sensitive consumers and a large group of loyal consumers for soju product or beer product as a whole. Moreover, we have to consider high level of SSNIP only if a hypothetical monopolist cannot make profits with 5–10% price increases. But the hypothetical monopolist can make profits with the normal 5–10% SSNIP in the present context, and we do not have to consider a higher level of price increase.

4.2.2. Estimation of actual sales loss and geographic market definition

Jeon et al. used Gallup Korea's survey data in estimating actual sales losses that result from increases in prices of soju and beer. Ryu and Yi instead used weekly date of sales in discount stores with bar codes. As KFTC decision noted, the data have a serious sample selection bias in that discount stores account for only 5% of total sales of soju and beer, and consumers who purchase soju and beer in discount outlets do not represent the whole population. Especially, the characteristics of consumers using discount outlets such as Carrefour may be different from those of usual consumers who buy soju and beer in drinking/dining places and other retail shops. On the other hand, a survey data can avoid such selection bias by constructing a sample which reflects the population of soju and beer consumers in terms of sex, age, education, job, income, region, etc. Gallup Korea conducted the survey with a sample of 1603 soju consumers and 1547 beer consumers in such a way that avoided selection bias.

http://dx.doi.org/10.5772/63225

Table 15 and **16** summarizes the results of our critical loss analyses:

	Actual loss vs. critical loss	Enlarge the product market beyond soju?
5% price increase	5.6 < 14.3%	*No*
10% price increase	10.6 < 25.0%	*No*

Table 15. Critical loss analysis for soju product.

	Actual loss vs. critical loss	Enlarge the product market beyond beer?
5% price increase	13.2 < 15.3%	*No*
10% price increase	22.1 < 26.5%	*No*

Table 16. Critical loss analysis for beer product.

These results show that product markets relevant to Hite-Jinro merger are two separate ones of soju and beer, not an integrated one of "pub alcoholic drink." A hypothetical monopolist of soju (beer) product can implement 5% and 10% price increases profitably. This means that soju and beer are not so close substitutes that both constitute a single product market in antitrust perspective.

Reinterpreting the actual losses in **Tables 15** and **16** in terms of elasticities, the price elasticity of soju is about 1.1 and that of beer is about 2.2–2.6. Previous empirical studies using actual data of soju and beer consumption shows the robustness of the results based on survey data. [23] Chung in [12] found that the own price elasticity of soju is in the range of 0.58–1.18 and that of beer is in the range of 0.94–1.31. And another Chung in [13] estimated the price elasticities of soju and beer as about 0.75–0.85 and 1.3–1.6, respectively. Given these estimates, our survey results seem to overstate consumers' response to price increases a little bit. However, the differences may not be so huge as to discredit the survey results after all. Furthermore, the critical loss analyses with the empirically estimated elasticities would support the conclusion even more strongly that soju and beer markets should be defined separately.

4.3. Critical loss analysis for geographic market definition

Given that soju and beer are separate products from a perspective of competition policy, Hite-Jinro merger is basically conglomerate. However, the merger contains a horizontal part since Hite has a subsidiary soju company, Hitejujo, in Chonbuk. Competitive evaluation of the horizontal part hinges on definition of the relevant geographic market. In the following I summarize the part of Jeon et al. on the definition of geographic soju market relevant to the horizontal merger between Hitejujo and Jinro. The starting point of analysis is Chonbuk area

[23] Unfortunately, we cannot cross-check the robustness of the results in **Tables 7** and **8** and **Tables 19** and **20** with empirical estimation of demands for disaggregated soju brands, not a whole soju product. That is mainly because it is not easy to obtain disaggregated data, and prices of all soju brands vary similarly without meaningful cross-sectional variances.

for which competitive concerns about the merger might be raised, and then it will be checked whether the relevant market should be enlarged further.

4.3.1. *Estimation of margins and critical loss*

We estimated the margins in the same way as before, in this case with Hitejujo and Jinro which account for more than 90% of sales in Chonbuk—42.5 and 50.6% in 2004, respectively (**Table 17**).

	Hitejujo (03 + 04)	Jinro (03 + 04)	Hitejujo + Jinro (03 + 04)
Sales (A)	37,054	1,309,026	1,346,080
Variable sales costs (B′)	17,894	656,014	673,909
Var. Mkt and Adm costs (C′)	12,411	261,109	275,780
Margin ratio ((A − B′ − C′)/A)	18.2%	29.9%	29.4%

Source: Companies' annual report.

Table 17. Margins of Hitejujo and Jinro in 2003 and 2004 (mil. won, %).

The margins of Hitejujo were lower than those of other soju producers, which was due to large expenses of marketing and administration. But the margins of the combined company were close to the average of soju industry since Hitejujo was very small in comparison with Jinro.

Critical losses, $CL = (X/(X + M))$, for $M = 29.4\%$ and $X = 5\%$, 10%, 20%, 30%, and 40% are as follows (**Table 18**):

	$X = 5\%$	$X = 10\%$	$X = 20\%$	$X = 30\%$
Critical loss	14.5%	25.5%	40.5%	50.5%

Table 18. Critical losses for the combined company of Hitejujo and Jinro.

We consider here high levels of SSNIP such as 20 and 30% in order to see whether there are a considerable number of consumers who show strong loyalty to local products as in the Moohak-Jinro case.

4.3.2. *Estimation of actual sales loss and geographic market definition*

Gallup Korea conducted a survey in 2005 with consumers in Chonbuk area for the analysis of their choice of soju products. The sample was selected to represent the average behavior of soju consumption in terms of sex, age, and regions, and the final 810 consumers were screened who responded that they usually consumed "Hite 2" (Hitejujo's brand name) or "Chamisle" (Jinro's brand name).[24]

The results of critical loss analyses are (**Tables 19** and **20**):

http://dx.doi.org/10.5772/63225

	Actual loss vs. critical loss	Enlarge the geographic market beyond Chonbuk?
5% increase	21.8 > 14.5%	Yes
10% increase	36.1 > 25.4%	Yes
20% increase	57.4 > 40.5%	Yes
30% increase	57.9 > 50.5%	Yes

Table 19. Critical loss analyses with data of dining/drinking houses.

	Actual loss vs. critical loss	Enlarge the geographic market beyond Chonbuk?
5% increase	20.7 > 14.5%	Yes
10% increase	37.0 > 25.4%	Yes
20% increase	52.2 > 40.5%	Yes
30% increase	54.9 > 50.5%	Yes

Table 20. Critical loss analyses with data of retailing shops.

These results show that Chonbuk consumers would switch their purchase of soju from their current main favorite brands to others to the extent that the relevant geographic market should not be confined to the Chonbuk region.

It still remains the issue of how far the geographic market should be enlarged, i.e., whether it is the country as a whole or some regions are excluded. To make a definite conclusion on this issue, we have to conduct further critical loss analyses. Instead, we made a tentative suggestion that the geographic market might be nationwide, excluding some southern regions such as Busan, Kyungnam, Kyungbuk, Chonnam, and Jeju. The main reason is that each of those regions has a dominant local producer and consumers with strong loyalty to a local product. Moreover, their current soju sales in Chonbuk are negligible. The KFTC also defined the geographic market relevant to the merger between Hitejujo and Jinro as "the country except Busan, Kyungnam, Kyungbuk, Chonnam, and Jeju."

It is to be noted that the market definition in an antitrust case is case-specific. In other words, it depends on a starting point of analysis, which is a product or a region for which competitive concerns are raised. The previous market definition in Moohak-Daesun was confined to Busan and Kyungnam since consumers in the region did not switch much their purchase from local products to products in other regions, e.g., Hitejujo and Jinro, in response to local price increases. On the other hand, there would be nothing wrong if the geographic market relevant to Hitejujo-Jinro had been extended to the whole country even including Busan and Kyungnam, even though it did not actually go that far. This does not involve any inconsistency, since consumers in two regions could have different preferences.

[24] Sampling error is 3.44% from 95% confidence interval.

Besides conducting critical loss analyses, we observe two facts that differentiate Hitejujo-Jinro from Moohak-Daesun. First, LIFO index in Chonbuk was only 42.5%, while that in Busan-Kyungnam was 94.7%. Compared to the conventional standard of 75–90% of LIFO-LOFI test, 40% must be too low. Second, there is a common pricing constraint in soju industry in that producers should apply the same wholesale price in the country. This suggests another basis of the national market in this case. One of the merging companies, Jinro, is a national producer which cannot raise soju price in Chonbuk without risking sales losses in other regions. On the other hand, both Moohak and Daesun are local producers which had virtually no other regions to consider in setting prices.

It is worthwhile to elaborate a bit more on why opposite conclusions were arrived at with respect to expanding the geographic market in the two cases of Moohak-Daesun and Hitejujo-Jinro. Notice that we tried to apply the same methods of critical loss analysis: e.g., the same classification of variable vs. fixed costs in deriving margins and the same construction of questionnaire in conducting surveys. Hence, the opposite results in two cases were tied to the idiosyncratic nature of the two geographic regions rather than the application of the test. People in Busan-Kyungnam have strong loyalty to their local brands, which have been rooted in the past history of local purchase requirement regulation and the political atmosphere aforementioned. On the other hand, people in Chonbuk are not so loyal to their local soju firms which are not indigenous anymore. Hitejujo and Jinro are hardly regarded as Chonbuk-based since Hite, a national beer company, acquired the former indigenous Chungbuk soju and Jinro is a national soju company. Furthermore, political regionalism in Chonbuk has not been as keen as Busan and Kyungnam since Chonbuk has never been a power center in recent Korean political history.

4.4. Implications for anticompetitive effects of Hite-Jinro merger

Since beer and soju are separate products, Hite-Jinro merger is a conglomerate one. KFTC considered four possible anticompetitive effects of the conglomerate merger in this case: (i) excluding competitors, (ii) strengthening entry barriers, (iii) limiting potential competitors, and (iv) raising prices. To alleviate concerns, the merger was given conditional approval. The imposed conditions of corrective measures included a price cap of RPI + 5% on Hite and Jinro's beer and soju, division of marketing workforce and organization of Hite and Jinro for five years, and some self-arrangement of not committing exclusionary practices in the future.

The first two concerns stem from the fact that beer and soju producers share the same distribution channels of liquor wholesale: Hite and Jinro accounted for 34.5% and 22.1% of liquor wholesalers' sales in 2004. It was alleged that the combination of two dominant companies in beer and soju could enhance its bargaining power against wholesalers and press them to influence final demands in favor of its brands. Moreover, strongholds of the two companies were different; Hite was dominant in southern provinces while Jinro was in Seoul and its adjacent regions. So the leverage effect of expanding monopoly powers across regions through tying or bundling was worried about by competitors of Hite and Jinro in beer and soju markets. [25] On the other hand, the defending party argued that pushing wholesalers or leveraging cannot be effective in the long run and that the ultimate determinant of final demands is consumer preference.[26] Jeon et al. conducted an econometric study which rejected the existence of leverage effects in previous mergers in beer and soju market (see [2]). The third concern of eliminating potential competitors is an often-claimed anticompetitive effect of conglomerate mergers. Lastly, the concern about raising prices is peculiar for conglomerate mergers. KFTC considered beer and soju as exerting some competitive constraints, even though it defined the two as different products. This sounds contradictory since market definition is nothing but a consideration of competitive constraints. A more practical basis for this concern was that the acquirer expended too much—over $3 billion dollars for the deal—and that it could not but increase product prices in order to resolve financial difficulties. Given the sunken nature of financial costs for the merger deal, the last concern does not seem to be warranted.

On the other hand, the KFTC did not consider the horizontal merger between Hitejujo and Jinro as restraining competition materially in the soju product market. Given the geographic market definition of the country as a whole except for five regions (Busan, Kyungnam, Kyungbuk, Chonnam, and Jeju), the market share of Hitejujo was merely 2.5%. The KFTC's merger guideline stipulates that anticompetitive concerns are insignificant if the gain of market share after the merger is less than 5% in the relevant market.

5. Conclusion

5.1. Recommendation

Several issues have been raised in the course of applying critical loss analysis in merger cases of Moohak-Daesun and Hite-Jinro. First of all, estimation of margins using accounting data involves some degree of discretionary or ad hoc classification of fixed and variable costs. The parties who defend an enlarged market definition argue for more fixed costs, and vice versa; it is because the larger the portion of fixed costs, the higher the rate of margins, and hence the lower the level of critical loss. The most controversial and significant components are labor costs and advertising expenses. The arguments of those who regard them as fixed are as follows: the time horizon in the SSNIP test is one year, and hiring regular workers and expensing advertising budgets do not vary in accordance of output changes within one year. But Seoul High Court and the KFTC interpreted the time horizon appropriate for SSNIP test as a significant period over which monopoly power can be exercised, which is not be confined to only one year. Given that, labor and advertising costs are not necessarily fixed.

Second, we used survey data in estimating price elasticities of consumer demand and actual losses corresponding to various levels of price increase in the SSNIP test. Economists usually prefer using actual historical data in estimating demands rather than resorting to survey data. However, in many cases we have data problems; data with the necessary degree of desegregation, time span, and representativeness are not available. Recent spread of bar code scanning

[25] See [14] for discussions of portfolio effects.

[26] Recent development in soju market seems to confirm this argument. Doosan recently emerged as a strong rival to Jinro with more than 10% market share in Seoul and its vicinities.

system in retailing shops, and consequent availability of POS (Point of Sale) data, is a promising development that may resolve data problems in the future.[27] But there are still many cases, such as Moohak-Daesun and Hite-Jinro, where POS data have a serious problem of sample selection bias in that they constitute a small portion of population data, and sample characteristics do not reflect those of the entire population. In such cases, a well executed survey can be a useful alternative source of data. Survey data are often discredited because questions tend to predetermine answers and that respondents tend to overstate (or understate) their responses. But questions in our survey are so straightforward that they do not risk predetermining answers; the questions simply ask how consumers will change purchases in cases of price increases. There still remains a problem of overstatement (or understatement) tendency. We have to take it into an appropriate account in drawing conclusions. Our results had considerable margins so that the conclusions were robust even after accounting such a tendency.

Third, we considered high price increases of 15 and 30% in the SSNIP test as well as conventional 5 and 10% in the Moohak-Daesun case. It was due to the fact that there were two groups of consumers in the regions—a price-sensitive one and another with loyalty to local brands. In such case, there is a concern that a local monopolist can exploit captured brand-loyal consumers by a high price strategy even though he cannot make profits with low prices. Of course, the usual criterion of 5–10% in the SSNIP test will be sufficient in most of cases where there are not many brand-loyal consumers.

Fourth, there is a subtle issue of how we should account income effect in price effects in hypothetical monopoly test. If the spirit is to include close demand substitutes in a relevant market, then we may have to focus substitution effect in price effects and to give less weight to actual losses due to income effect. On the other hand, if the spirit is to identify a set of products and regions for which a monopolist can exercise market power, then we have to consider both substitution and income effects equally. US and EU guidelines are not clear about which is the right perspective, while the current version of the KFTC merger guideline seems to be based on the former.

The last remark is on case specificity and possible asymmetry of market definition. That is, market definition in antitrust cases is case-specific; it depends on the starting point of analysis, from which we check whether the relevant market should be enlarged further. There would be nothing wrong if the geographic market relevant Moohak-Daesun was confined to Busan and Kyungnam, while the market relevant to Hitejujo and Jinro had been extended to the whole country including Busan and Kyungnam. Similarly, there would be nothing wrong if a critical loss analysis starting from soju product implied that soju was a separate market while an analysis starting from beer product had implied that beer and soju were in the same market, even though it did not turn out that way. Such possibilities do not involve any inconsistency, since consumers in two regions, or of two products, could have different preferences, and their consumption behaviors could result in asymmetric cross-elasticities.

[27] POS data have already played an important role in antitrust econometrics in a well-known US merger case of Staples-Office Depot in 1997 and a recent Korean retailing merger case of Eland-Carrefour in 2006. See [15] and [16].

5.2. Further study

Critical loss analysis is a convenient tool for practical market definition, and it proved to be very useful and successful in the two cases examined in the paper. Unfortunately, however, there are not many industries for which the analysis can be actually implemented. Soju and beer industries in Korea are rather special in that companies in these industries focus on basically one liquor business, which enable us to calculate the ratio of margins with public accounting data. Also there are not many different products in the industries, for which we can survey consumers' purchasing behavior. On the other hand, it is practically impossible to conduct critical loss analysis for industries with too many businesses and products, for example, retailing or banking industry. For those industries, the SSNIP test will remain just as a conceptual framework without a quantitative support of critical loss analysis.

Acknowledgements

This work was supported by the National Research Foundation of Korea Grant funded by the Korean Government (NRF-2013S1A3A2053586).

Author details

Jeon Seonghoon*

Address all correspondence to: jeonsh@sogang.ac.kr

Department of Economics, Sogang University, Seoul, South Korea

References

[1] Jeon S, Shin K. An economic analysis of geographic market definition relevant to Moohak-Daesun merger. The Korean Journal of Industrial Organization. 2006; 14: 17–66. (in Korean language).

[2] Jeon S. The method and cases of market definition for the purpose of competition policies: Hite-Jinro merger in 2005. Journal of Korean Economic Studies. 2007; 19: 75–115. (in Korean language).

[3] Werden G. The 1982 merger guidelines and the ascent of the hypothetical monopolist paradigm. Antitrust Law Journal. 2003; 71: 253–275.

[4] U.S. DOJ and FTC, Horizontal merger guidelines. 2010; 1–34.

[5] European Commission, Commission notice on the definition of the relevant market for the purposes of community competition law. Official Journal of the European Communities. 1997; C 372: 5–13.

[6] Harris B, Simons J. Focusing on market definition: How much substitution is necessary? Research in Law and Economics. 1989; 12: 207–226.

[7] Katz M, Shapiro C. Critical loss: Let's tell the whole story. Antitrust. 2003; 17: 49–56.

[8] Church J, Ware R. Industrial Organization: A Strategic Approach. Boston: Irwin McGraw-Hill; 2000. 926 p.

[9] Choi J, Hong S, Jeon S. Local identity and persistent leadership in market share dynamics: Evidence from deregulation in the Korean soju industry. The Korean Economic Review. 2013; 29: 267–304.

[10] Elzinga K, Hogarty T. The problem of geographic market delineation in antimerger suits. Antitrust Bulletin.1973; 18: 45–81.

[11] Ryu K, Yi S. Economic analysis of effects of Hite's takeover of Jinro on competition in liquor market. Consulting Project Report for OB Beer. 2005. (in Korean language)

[12] Chung J. SSNIP test and estimation of demand for the domestic liquor market – Hite-Jinro case [M.A. thesis]. Seoul: Sogang University; 2006. (in Korean language)

[13] Chung P. The effects on demand for alcoholic drinks and revenue in Korea. Korean Journal of Economics. 2005; 15: 36–57. (in Korean language)

[14] Watson P. Portfolio effects in EC merger law. Antitrust Bulletin. 2003; 48: 781–805.

[15] Dalkir S, Warren-Boulton F. Prices. Market Definition, and the Effects of Merger: Staples-Office Depot (1997). In: Kwoka J, White L, editors. The Antitrust Revolution: Economics, Competition, and Policy. 6th ed. New York: Oxford Univ. Press. 2014. p. 166–193.

[16] Jeon S, Whang Y. An econometric analysis of competitive effects of Eland-Carrefour merger in 2006. Journal of Regulation Studies. 2010; 19: 75–103. (in Korean language)

Chapter 6

A Comparison between the Presence and Absence of Regulation in the Spanish Electricity Market

Victor M. F. Moutinho, António C. Moreira and Jorge H. Mota

Additional information is available at the end of the chapter

http://dx.doi.org/10.5772/62953

Abstract

There is an important gap in the literature on the promotion of competition in electricity markets in what pertains to the analysis of two different streams: the absence and presence of regulation. Accordingly, the main objective of this study is to analyze the interactions among market power indexes, marginal costs, and bidding strategies in the two mentioned scenarios, for comparative purposes. The methodology used is based on panel cointegration methods. The results point to the significant inclusion of different bidding strategies in the retail market: (i) fuel prices exercise a differential impact on the power plants' marginal costs, (ii) the marginal costs have a significantly positive effect on quantity sold and on net quantity, and (iii) the market power measures under regulation have a significantly positive long-term impact on the quantity sold and a negative impact on net quantity supplied in wholesale market. Although there is some literature on this issue, the main novelty of this article is the discussion of the regulatory implications that could have been adopted in order to control and mitigate the market power, to encourage new investments in new technologies, and to recover sunk costs with the transition to a competitive market.

Keywords: market power, marginal costs, regulation, competition, panel cointegration

1. Introduction

Reforms in the Spanish electric sector, as well as in other European countries, Consisted fundamentally on the transition of a vertically integrated system comprising production, transportation, distribution, and commercialization of energy to a system that splits them into two main large groups: one group with regulated, noncompetitive activities such as transportation and distribution of energy and another with competitive, nonregulated activities such as production and commercialization of energy. This split-up aimed at increasing economic efficiency through price adjustments (short-term objectives) and at improving investment decisions, seeking to optimize the risks of those very same investments (long-term objectives).

In Spain, the total electricity output consists mainly of thermal power, hydroelectricity, and nuclear power. Thermal power accounts for over 80% of the total generating capacity while hydroelectricity accounts for around 15%. As a result, oil and coal prices changes strongly affect main industry players of the electric power industry. In order to face this problem, since 1997, Spain has gradually liberalized the electricity market so that the prices of fuel, gas, and coal fully reflect the costs of the production and of the costs of natural and environmental resources.

Hence, technologies with high fixed costs and low variable costs operate almost continuously in time and their payback is determined by the hourly prices set throughout the year. In the case of technologies with high variable costs whose production is discontinuous and reliant on exogenous variables, such as hydraulicity or wind speed, the market picks up one or other technology by unpredictable events leading to production yields turnouts. This adjustment is not possible in the electrical power industry because (a) most of the turnouts are not replicable and (b) the existence of sunk costs encourages the rejection of technologies whose payback is not enough to cover average costs but just the variable costs; therefore, it is unlikely for customers to pay electricity at the market price and that would be a required condition for the capacity reduction and adjustment.

Theory suggests that within the electrical power industry, both plant or grid level, when one fuel is substituted by another, there is a comovement in the commodity prices. In thermal power plants, fuel cost is the largest cost, accounting for 70% of the variable costs. The rise in coal prices, especially the coal price for electricity generation, directly increases the electrical producers operating costs and reduces corporate profits. As a consequence of high price increases, many electric power firms were confronted with heavy losses. As a result, in order to improve the operating conditions of electric power firms, the price of electricity increased to alleviate the coal–electricity price contradiction.

The Spanish electricity spot market pricing is characterized by a certain degree of nonconstant volatility and a strong seasonality. The fluctuation of demand over time, as a result of the optimal mix of production technologies, causes the electricity market to favor based-load plants with low variable costs. In this case, electric grid players, in order to recover fixed costs, tend to withhold their production as long as they can so that their revenues are higher than the lost opportunity costs.

As the supply function of the electrical system includes a wide variety of technologies, the market yields low rewards for some technologies and high rewards for others—e.g., some technologies with high fixed costs and low variable costs operate almost continuously and other technologies with high variable costs operate discontinuously. As a consequence, neither investments in different technologies nor adjustments to demands are easily replicable. In

http://dx.doi.org/10.5772/62953

addition, sunk costs discourage the abandonment of technologies whose remuneration does not cover average costs, only the variable ones.

The market price corresponds that way to a marginal price, in the way that it would be the price of which an extra unit of energy would be rewarded if the charge value would increase of one unit. This price corresponds to the latest offered price by the last generator to be dispatched on the pool, with that very same generator assuming a big market power, specifically when the difference between installed production capacity and network charge is reduced.

The existence of different kinds of agents in the market with different sizes, organization, and knowledge can lead to situations of asymmetric information (adverse selection) or even to collusive behaviors, creating favorable conditions to the existence of market power, with its elapsed consequences for social welfare.

From the supply side, the reduced number of companies can lead to strategic oligopolistic behaviors. This possibility is even worsened when demand increases leading companies to fight for markets shares.

As the different technologies of the supply function of the electricity market lead to specific price–quantity pairs for each of the 24 h of the following day, the aggregation of the bids of all power plants owned by a single generator allows for the obtainment of its hourly supply schedule. As a result, the quantity–price pair should be a point on its supply schedule. This procedure can continue as long as the number of possible realization of residual demand is not higher than the number of steps in the supply function. Therefore, the expected profit maximizing supply schedule should pass through all expost profit maximizing price and quantity pairs [1, 2].

With an increasing concentration index and inelastic demand, producers are more willing to set prices well above marginal costs. Although in the presence of market concentration most models would predict prices above marginal cost, market conditions, regulation of electricity auction rules may strongly influence margins [1]. According to Ciarreta and Espinosa [2, 3], the sustainability of the Spanish electricity market was threatened by the difficulty in controlling market power and by an increasing reliance on bidding strategies in the spot market.

Between 2002 and 2006, Endesa and Iberdrola's large power production installed capacity vis-à-vis the global capacity of the Spanish market, as well as their pricing capacity in the wholesale market, gave them the market power in the electricity market. Moreover, the pool pricing offered throughout the different hourly periods was conditioned mainly by the differences between production technologies used by the power plants that generate the installed system.

In the Spanish market, as any normal oligopolist, Endesa had an incentive to underproduce, in order to raise the price received for the net electricity sold to the market, whereas Iberdrola overproduced due to an oligopsonistic incentive to reduce the price paid for the infra-marginal units purchased from the spot market. Due to Endesa's "net supplier" and Iberdrola's "net demander" behavior, Kühn and Machado [4] claim that market power might be exercised according to the firms' behavior as net demanders or net suppliers.

In line with this, this article aims at contributing to the analysis and evaluation of the market power exercise in which we propose to formulate and validate a conceptual model in which electricity companies will develop their actions without resorting to cooperation. The market equilibrium is deduced from a behavioral model analysis, via conjectural variations model, in which prices are external variables set by the market, businesses take decisions regarding the quantity to produce for each price levels taking into account that their decisions will affect the others and others' decisions will affect theirs.

Vertical integration between generation (liberalized) and distribution (regulated) neutralized market power [1–3] as distribution surplus was used for the Costs of Transition to Competition, namely CTC payments.

Although Endesa and Iberdrola's should have behaved as net sellers (to promote competition), as any positive surplus generated by a distribution company was shared among the generators according to percentages given by the CTC rights, incentives of vertically integrated firms to change prices determined they behave as net buyers or net sellers [4]. The incentives provided by the regulation led to lower prices than the ones predicted by the profit maximization behavior. Moreover, the CTC payment was conditional on an average pool price not higher than 36.06 €/MWh. If the electricity producer average price exceeded that amount the revenues obtained for the higher price were subtracted from future CTC payments [2].

The main purpose of this study is to empirically investigate the three following questions:

i. Do fossil fuel prices and market power exercise a significant positive effect on marginal costs? To answer this question, we use a panel cointegration estimation of a regression model with marginal costs per power plant as the dependent variable, the fossil fuel prices are used as explanatory variables, and the two measures of market power, in the absence and in the presence of regulation, as a control variables;

ii. Do marginal costs cause or improve bidding strategies of electricity generators? To answer this question, we use the panel cointegration estimation of a regression model with quantity sold in the wholesale market as the dependent variable, marginal costs per power plant and the two measure of market power in the absence and in the presence regulation are used as explanatory variables. Purchased quantity to sell in open market is used as a control variable.

iii. Do marginal costs cause or improve net quantities transactioned by electricity generators? To answer this question, we use the panel cointegration estimation of a regression model with net quantities as the dependent variable, the marginal cost per power plant is used as explanatory variable, and the measure of market power in the absence and under regulation are used as a control variable.

The quantitative evaluation of the two proposed models regarding the strategic behavior of the Spanish electricity companies allows to observe carefully the market power issue displayed by electricity companies and, on the other hand, the tacit coordination or collusion between electrical companies, in that each company knows exactly how and when their rivals change their quantities allowing them to change interdependently their sold and purchased quantities

http://dx.doi.org/10.5772/62953

in the pool market in order to maintain supply levels which grant them high profits. Therefore, the main objective of this article is to examine and validate the type of strategic behavior of every Spanish electric company and consequent influence in the market power resulting from the type of decision variable considered in the profit maximization and still empirically verify the analysis period considered if that strategic behavior is linked with the will of the electric companies to control the market or increase its market power decreasing that way the competitiveness effect.

After this brief introduction, the rest of the paper is structured as follows: the Section 2 provides the literature review. Section 3 describes the data and methodology used in the empirical analysis. Section 4 describes the econometric strategy and presents the empirical results. Section 5 concludes with some policy implications.

2. Literature review

Wholesale electricity markets have been analyzed over time, especially in deregulated markets as there are strong incentives to maximize profits taking advantages of low cost production.

Market power has also been under scrutiny, as several methodologies, approaches and conceptualizations have been used to avoid this problem. For example, Neuhoff et al. [5], based on Cournot models analyzed how regulatory mechanism in the transmission network influence market equilibrium.

The use of the supply function equilibrium has been used with linear marginal costs [6] and with constant marginal costs [7] to address the electricity supply market function. On the other hand, Fabra, Von der Fehr and Harbord [8] demonstrated that market power may be present in multiunit auction models.

The study of the Californian wholesale electricity market [9–11] provided good insights for the analysis of the wholesale market inefficiencies.

The Spanish market has also been subject to important analysis in recent years [2, 3, 12–14].

Furió and Lucia [12] analyzed the particularities of the Spanish intra-day market bidding behavior and concluded that some power generators have a clear economic incentive to be called up in the subsequent transmission constraints resolution process and avoid being dispatched in the day-ahead market.

Based on the different bidding behavior of large and small generators, Ciarreta and Espinosa [3] provided a measure of market power at different competitive levels explaining the reason why equilibrium prices are above the reference marginal costs, and finding that in the day-ahead market larger generators are able to increase prices well above the competitive benchmark.

Ciarreta and Espinosa [2] measured the gap between optimal price in the absence of regulation and real prices when analyzing the impact of regulation on the electricity wholesale market from 2002 to 2005. They concluded that the regulation affected wholesale prices considerably, but at the beginning of 2006 became less effective due to changes introduced in the regulatory regime.

The market power exercise was also analyzed by Kühn and Machado [4], who demonstrated, using a two-step GMM econometric estimation, that the two major operators of the Spanish market (Endesa and Iberdrola) used the CTC payments to increase or decrease prices, according to their behavior as net buyers and net sellers in the market. Similarly, Fabra and Toro [15] also analyzed market power in the Spanish market, specifically the price formation in price-war stages and in collusion periods. They concluded that in price-war periods, Endesa's mark-up is negative while Iberdrola's is positive. On the other hand, in collusion periods, both firms had positive margins, which is a clear indication of market power exercise. Fabra and Toro [15] have also recognized the coexistence of low prices coordinated with mixed price strategies, which leads to multiple price equilibrium.

Moutinho, Vieira, and Moreira [16] addressed the long-term relationship between spot electricity market price and commodity prices using cointegration techniques. They conclude that the prices of fuel and the prices of Brent are intertwined as the latter tend to re-establish the price equilibrium.

The coexistence of competition in the electricity spot market and the CTC regulatory compensation mechanism is not compatible [17]. Although this situation leads to a decrease in prices, this study reveals that its joint existence enhances the power market exercise as it leads to an increase of the equilibrium price. Inadequate payments can promote both production inefficiency and delay or prevent new competition.

When discussing the factors that influence energy efficiency, conservation decisions, and the most appropriate policies for their promotion, Linares and Labandeira [18] claim that energy conservation policies are required. They propose the provision of information to consumers as well as economic instruments.

A generation-expansion model involving CO_2 emissions trading and green certificates was developed by Linares et al. [19]. Taking into account firms' oligopolistic behavior, they tried to respond to the needs of firms and regulators in electricity markets.

In the body of literature debating, the impact of wholesale price caps on investment in oligopolistic electricity markets, Grobman and Carey [20], Stoft [21], and Joskow and Tirole [22] study the long-term effects of price caps on investment in new generation units under different market structures. Biglaiser and Riordan [23] study the dynamics of price regulation for an industry adjusting to exogenous technological change. They show that price cap regulation leads to more efficient capital replacement decisions when compared to rate-of-return regulation.

Strategic real options models have been developed by combining real options arguments with differential games in order to model investment in oligopolistic industries [24–26]. More recently, Earle et al. [27] use a one time period model of Cournot competition with uncertain demand to show that price cap regulation in the presence of uncertainty might fail to increase production and therefore fail to increase consumer welfare.

3. Data, econometric methods, and results

In order to test the relationships that may exist between marginal costs, fossil fuel prices, net set selling quantities, and market power indexes in the Spanish OMEL (Operador del Mercado Ibérico de Energía) wholesale market, a rationalized cointegration analysis is going to be applied on a set of cross-firms panel data. Panel cointegration tests, panel unit root tests, and dynamic panel causality tests are going to be conducted to confirm the validity of the panel data model estimation.

The error correction model (ECM) is a linear regression equation that provides a description of the possible nature of interdependence of the short-run movements of the cointegrated variables under study, namely, marginal costs, and sets of bids quantities supplied from hydro-electrical, nuclear, coal, combined-cycle gas turbine, and fuel-oil power plants.

In this article, five panel tests are going to be run: Levin, Lin, and Chu test [28] (hereafter, LLC), Breitung test [29], Hadri test [30], Im, Pesaran, and Shin test [31] (hereafter, IPS), and ADF-Fischer test. While the first three assume a common unit root, the last two assume individual unit root process across the cross-sections.

3.1. Data and specification of variables

The marginal costs of power generation were obtained for all power plants in the portfolio. Then, plants were ranked in order of their ascending marginal costs as produced, in their quest for profit-maximization and start their production from the plant with lowest marginal cost. Based on the merit-order effect, plants are brought on line to meet increasing demand. Theoretically, daily changes in fuel and carbon prices can change the merit order through their effect on relative marginal costs of power generation.

The data of the demand and supply of Endesa, Iberdrola, Unión Fenosa, Hidrocantabrico, Viesgo, and other fringe competitive groups were gathered on a daily basis. A 24 h moving average was calculated for each production unit in the Spanish wholesale electricity market. Data regarding each agent of the wholesale electricity market were retrieved from OMEL database. Information regarding market prices, quantity offered, and quantity purchased to sell in open market was obtained from January 2002 until June 2006.

We adopted the expression of the marginal costs of a power plant given by Lagarto et al. [32]: $MC_{p,fuel} = \frac{f \times cf}{LHV \times \eta_p}$, in which $MC_p = MC_{p,fuel}$; $MC_{p,fuel}$ is the marginal cost of fossil fuel of power plant p in Euros/; MWh MC_p is the marginal cost of power plant $p$in €/MWh; the Lower Heating Value in kcal/t is represented by LHV; 859,845 kcal/MWh represents the conversion factor cf; f is the fossil fuel price in €s/t; and η_p is power plant efficiency in %. The daily periods analyzed were significantly conditioned by the differences among the various production technologies used by the power plants. We used the daily spot prices of fuel, coal and gas to compute the marginal costs. Data of major fuel sources (oil, coal, and gas) were retrieved from the Energy Systems database of a university research center. The unitary marginal costs of the nuclear and hydroelectric technologies are the ones referred in Ciarreta and Espinosa [1].

For measuring the market power under the absence of regulation (Lerner Index 1) the following expression was used: $(P_{OMEL} - cmg)/P_{OMEL}$, according to Ciarreta and Espinosa [3]. For measuring the market power under the presence of regulation (Price cap equal to 36.06 €/ MWh), we used the Lerner index 2, given by: $(P_{OMEL} - P_{cap})/P_{cap}$.

3.2. Previous analysis: the impact of marginal costs by technology on mark-up

The supply of electricity follows peculiar characteristics as the marginal costs associated with the production of electricity depends on the technology being used. Fuel prices influence the production cost of electric power plants, as to produce electricity these plants are used in merit order, i.e., available power plants are used to generate electricity based on the ascending order of price. In this situation, the producer offers positive net-supply with positive mark-ups and pushes down the price using its market power, while mark-ups are zero at the contracting point where net-supply is also zero [33].

In this previous analysis, it is relevant to explain the relationship between the variable mark-up and independent variables, whose multiplicative and qualitative effects will be measured by multiplying the marginal costs by the technology at the stock market closing time. This differentiation will be processed using binary variables, which assume a unitary value if, at the $hour_i$ of the stock market closing time, the technology "j" is considered zero; otherwise j = 1 = coal, 2 = hydraulic, 3 = fuel oil, 4 = fuel gas, 5 = nuclear, and 6 = gas combined cycle.

By analyzing the "*F*" statistic, one can conclude that the individual effects of each electricity firm, represented by the constant, are not all equal as assumed in the "Pooled" model. Instead, they are different as assumed in the "Fixed Effect" model. The interpretation of this test is that the specificities of each electricity company are important to explain the increase of the marginal costs causal OMEL mark-up.

As presented in **Table 1**, one can conclude that there is an average decrease in the mark-up of €0.5608 for the set of the electricity companies considered in the study, when marginal costs vary one unit using coal, regarding the remaining technologies. When using hydraulic technology at stock market closing time at peak hours, the impact of the variation of one unit on the marginal costs induces an average increase of €0.1479 in the mark-up of all electricity producers. One can witness that a unitary increase in the marginal costs using fuel oil technology induces an average decrease of € 0.33534 units in the mark-up regarding the remaining technologies. The average decrease in the mark-up would be €0.2925 when fuel gas is used as technology and €0.3803 for the gas combined cycle for all the electricity producers when marginal costs vary one unit *ceteris paribus*.

Overall, the main evidence of the characteristics of those different production technologies is that coal plants set the prices mainly on the low demand periods, while hydroelectric plants prevail during peak hours. Consequently, since Endesa provides near 57% of electricity production generated from coal, while Iberdrola leads hydraulic adjustable production, both companies set the marginal price in the market. Finally, Endesa and Iberdrola play the role of pivot companies in the Spanish wholesale market. Their capacity is at least equal to the market's existing idle supply, especially during the peak demand periods.

	Pooled	Fixed effect	Random effect
Dcmg1	–0.51469	–0.5608	–0.548427
	(0.0070)	(0.007472)	(0.007359)
Dcmg2	0.165627	0.14790	0.154585
	(0.057316)	(0.05709)	(0.05714)
Dcmg3	–0.335053	–0.33534	–0.332651
	(0.005512)	(0.0060)	(0.00591)
Dcmg4	–0.30791	–0.29251	–0.29770
	(0.004286)	(0.004355)	(0.004346)
Dcmg6	–0.41119	–0.38030	–0.38789
	(0.00663)	(0.006761)	(0.006727)
Constant	1.940205	1.97557	1.96954
	(0.0013567)	(0.01383)	(0.01621)
F	1260.3	1248.9	
P | Z |			0.000

Table 1. The impact of the marginal costs, by technology, on the Mark-Up.

The abovementioned behavior of the main two firms of the Spanish electricity market opens a window of opportunity to address the relationship between competition and regulation. Although an expanding body of literature exists on the promotion of competition in electricity markets, there is an important gap in analyzing it in two different scenarios: the absence and presence of regulation. In such a way this study analyzes the interactions among market power indexes, marginal costs, and bidding strategies in the two mentioned scenarios. There are differences in pricing behavior between larger and smaller generators in the Spanish wholesale market. Given that demand is very inelastic and supply highly concentrated, larger generators, such as, Endesa and Iberdrola seem to be able to increase prices by a considerable amount, especially in peak hours.

As Vives [34] states, mark-ups decrease if producers have access to the same information, such as the expected signs in the behavior of market prices and marginal costs, potentially correlated. In the case of duopoly in the Spanish electricity market, Endesa and Iberdrola are able to increase or decrease the bid price, involving large amounts of kwh, given the sharing of information between the spot market and the open market, which might have underpinned the collusive behavior of these two players and their followers. This may justify the increase or decrease of mark-ups, or pushed toward an increase or decrease of the market price and marginal cost, explaining in this way the high or low prices in the market. However, for Ciarreta [35] not only the vertical integration of production and distribution activities explains a higher margin of cost-price for Iberdrola than for Endesa, but also it is plausible to admit the reversibility of this cost–price evolution, stressing that market power mitigation may be sustained by the threat of new regulation and the entry of new players in the market, as was expected with the liberalization process which involves a greater incentive to competition in the production of electricity. On the other hand, the recovery of sunk costs with the CTC mechanism provides different incentives for different players. It is expected that in the OMEL market, there are new conditions for estimating accurately the production marginal costs per technology for, given the historic hourly quantity bids on the market by technology type.

After this previous analysis, in the next section, the main purpose of this econometric study is to answer the three questions described in introduction, in which panel cointegration estimation of a regression model is used under the absence and in the presence of regulation.

Tests assuming a common unit root process				**Test assuming individual unit root process**
Series name	LLC t^*-stat: H_0: Unit root	Breitung t-stat: H_0: Unit root	Hadri Z-stat: H_0: No Unit root	IPS W-t-bar stat: H_0: Unit root
Quantity purchased to sell in open market	–6.5448 [0.9950]	–7.3201*** [0.0000]	21.2876*** [0.0000]	–3.4255*** [0.0003]
Coal price	–3.2588*** [0.0000]	–4.0808*** [0.0000]	34.9151*** [0.0000]	–5.5105*** [0.0000]
Fuel-oil price	–4.7158 [0.7254]	–0.4339 [0.3322]	48.5190*** [0.0000]	0.7321 [0.7680]
Gas price	–6.8977 [0.8823]	–3.1011*** [0.0010]	19.8958*** [0.0000]	–3.3736*** [0.0004]
Sold Quantity	–4.3792* [0.0997]	–5.7878*** [0.0000]	30.1633*** [0.0000]	–2.2015** [0.0139]
Marginal cost	–4.5782 [1.000]	–16.3918*** [0.0000]	25.4702*** [0.0000]	–4.8489*** [0.0000]
Net quantity	–7.2965 [1.0000]	–8.4103*** [0.0000]	17.5772*** [0.0000]	–8.0987*** [0.0000]
Lerner index 1	–5.9166 [1.0000]	–18.6325*** [0.0000]	19.4469*** [0.0000]	–7.9349*** [0.0000]
Lerner index 2	–8.1611 [0.9791]	–7.7131*** [0.0000]	15.3261*** [0.0000]	–6.7004*** [0.0000]

Notes: *, ** and *** represent significance at the 10%, 5%, and 1% levels, respectively.

Table 2. Panel unit root tests results.

3.3. Panel unit root tests

Panel data is generally characterized by unobserved heterogeneity with parameters that are cross-section specific. In some cases, it is not appropriate to consider independent cross-section units. The rejection of the null hypothesis of Panel unit root tests is difficult to interpret because it means that a significant fraction of cross-section units is stationary, although there is no explicit quantification of the size of this fraction.

Panel unit root tests are often grouped into two main categories: first-generation tests, which assume cross-sectional independence [31, 36, 37]; and second generation tests, which explicitly allow for some form of cross-section dependence [38]. This article applies panel unit root tests to ascertain whether or not the time series of each variable included in the Autoregressive Distributed Lag (ADL) contained a stochastic trend and to test whether the set of variables are stationary or not.

The panel unit root test is based on the following autoregressive specification [39]: $y_{it} = \rho_i \cdot y_{it-1} + \Delta_i \cdot X_{it} + \mu_{it}$, where $i = 1, 2, \ldots, N$ represents companies observed over periods, $t = 1, 2, \ldots, T$. X_{it} are exogenous variables in the model including individual deterministic effects, such as constants (fixed effects) and linear time trends, which capture cross-sectional heterogeneity, and ρ_i are the autoregressive coefficients. If $\rho_i < 1$, y_i it is said to be weakly trend-stationary. Conversely, if $\rho_i = 1$, then y_i contains a unit root; μ_{it} is the stationary error terms.

To test that all individual series of the panel contain a unit root, we use LLC, Breitung, IPS, and Hadri tests [28–31]. It tests the null hypothesis of data being stationary versus the alternative hypothesis in which at least one panel contains a unit root. The results of panel tests are difficult to interpret if the null hypothesis is rejected. In the LLC and IPS tests, cross-sectional means are subtracted to minimize problems arising from cross-section dependence.

Table 2 reports unit root tests for the following variables: quantity purchased in wholesale market to sell in open market, coal price, fuel-oil price, gas price, marginal cost, net quantity, Lerner index under absence (Lerner Index 1), and presence (Lerner Index 2) of regulation. The regressions contain an intercept and a time trend.

The LLC test rejects the presence of a unit root under significantly weaker evidence for the following variables: coal price and sold quantity. The Hadri test has a different (stationary) null hypothesis and provides strong evidence that all panels have a unit root. The Breitung and IPS tests cannot reject the presence of unit root in fuel-oil price.

Although there are cases in which the null hypothesis was rejected, it is possible to assume nonstationarity of the series, which holds the possibility of long-term relationships between the variables. Moreover, it is possible to include the variables in the cointegration study in which the null hypothesis was rejected in the following situations: first, assuming that they are first-order integrated and, second, when the panel test does not show such results due to the high probability of cross-section correlation.

3.4. Panel cointegration tests

After assuring nonstationarity, we used the methodology proposed by Engle and Granger [40] to test the cointegration hypothesis of the series as used afterward [41–44].

Pedroni [41] uses the residuals from the static long-run regression to construct seven panel cointegration tests: four of them assuming the homogeneity of the AR term, whereas the remaining tests are less restrictive, as they allow for heterogeneity of the AR term.

The statistics based on the homogeneous alternative hypothesis consist on pooled type estimates, or within-groups statistics [42]. When considering the heterogeneous alternative hypothesis, test statistics are formed by means of the estimated individual values for each panel unit *i*, which Pedroni [42] calls between-groups estimators.

This study relies on the Westerlund [43] test that suggests four cointegration tests that are based on structural rather than residual dynamics and allow for a large degree of heterogeneity. They test the null hypothesis by inferring if the error correction term is equal to zero. The null hypothesis of no cointegration is rejected in the case of rejection of the null hypothesis of no error correction [44]. Two tests are designed with an alternative hypothesis that the panel is cointegrated as a whole, while the other two test the alternative hypotheses that there is at least one individual series that is cointegrated. Each test is able to accommodate individual firm specific short-run dynamics, including serially correlated error terms and nonstrictly exogenous regressors, individual specific intercept, and trend terms, as well as individual-specific slope parameters.

As the relationship among the variables may be spurious even if the series are nonstationary, it is necessary to perform panel cointegration tests to make sure that there is indeed a long-term relationship.

As shown in **Table 3**, the results do provide strong support for the presence of cointegration, according to Pedroni's test statistics. However, the results of the Westerlund's test, as provided by the cross-sections, provide evidence of cointegration further indicating the possibility of a bidirectional long-run equilibrium relationship between marginal costs and the supply strategy. This is consistent across the different cases: in the absence or presence of regulation.

To test that all individual series of the panel contain a unit root, we use LLC, Breitung, IPS, and Hadri tests [28–31]. It tests the null hypothesis of data being stationary versus the alternative hypothesis in which at least one panel contains a unit root. The results of panel tests are difficult to interpret if the null hypothesis is rejected. In the LLC and IPS tests, cross-sectional means are subtracted to minimize problems arising from cross-section dependence.

Table 2 reports unit root tests for the following variables: quantity purchased in wholesale market to sell in open market, coal price, fuel-oil price, gas price, marginal cost, net quantity, Lerner index under absence (Lerner Index 1), and presence (Lerner Index 2) of regulation. The regressions contain an intercept and a time trend.

The LLC test rejects the presence of a unit root under significantly weaker evidence for the following variables: coal price and sold quantity. The Hadri test has a different (stationary) null hypothesis and provides strong evidence that all panels have a unit root. The Breitung and IPS tests cannot reject the presence of unit root in fuel-oil price.

Although there are cases in which the null hypothesis was rejected, it is possible to assume nonstationarity of the series, which holds the possibility of long-term relationships between the variables. Moreover, it is possible to include the variables in the cointegration study in which the null hypothesis was rejected in the following situations: first, assuming that they are first-order integrated and, second, when the panel test does not show such results due to the high probability of cross-section correlation.

3.5. Panel cointegration tests

After assuring nonstationarity, we used the methodology proposed by Engle and Granger [40] to test the cointegration hypothesis of the series as used afterward [41–44].

Pedroni [41] uses the residuals from the static long-run regression to construct seven panel cointegration tests: four of them assuming the homogeneity of the AR term, whereas the remaining tests are less restrictive, as they allow for heterogeneity of the AR term.

The statistics based on the homogeneous alternative hypothesis consist on pooled type estimates, or within-groups statistics [42]. When considering the heterogeneous alternative hypothesis, test statistics are formed by means of the estimated individual values for each panel unit i, which Pedroni [42] calls between-groups estimators.

This study relies on the Westerlund [43] test that suggests four cointegration tests that are based on structural rather than residual dynamics and allow for a large degree of heterogeneity. They test the null hypothesis by inferring if the error correction term is equal to zero. The null hypothesis of no cointegration is rejected in the case of rejection of the null hypothesis of no error correction [44]. Two tests are designed with an alternative hypothesis that the panel is cointegrated as a whole, while the other two test the alternative hypotheses that there is at least one individual series that is cointegrated. Each test is able to accommodate individual firm specific short-run dynamics, including serially correlated error terms and nonstrictly exogenous regressors, individual specific intercept, and trend terms, as well as individual-specific slope parameters.

As the relationship among the variables may be spurious even if the series are nonstationary, it is necessary to perform panel cointegration tests to make sure that there is indeed a long-term relationship.

As shown in **Table 3**, the results do provide strong support for the presence of cointegration, according to Pedroni's test statistics. However, the results of the Westerlund's test, as provided by the cross-sections, provide evidence of cointegration further indicating the possibility of a bidirectional long-run equilibrium relationship between marginal costs and the supply strategy. This is consistent across the different cases: in the absence or presence of regulation.

	Westerlund	Pedroni			
$Equation\,1A: MC_{it} = \beta_0 + \beta_1 CoalP_{it} + \beta_2 FuOlP_{it} + \beta_3 GasP_{it} + \beta_4 LerI_{noRegit} + \varepsilon_{it}$	G_T –4.241*** [0.002]	Panel v-Statistic	–0.0945 [0.537]	Group rho-Statistic	–56.190*** [0.000]
	G_α –68.228*** [0.000]	Panel rho-Statistic	–52.863*** [0.000}	Group PP-Statistic	–28.698*** [0.000]
	P_T –9.472** [0.012]	Panel PP-Statistic	–26.606*** [0.000]	Group ADF-Statistic	–3.308***[0.000]
	P_α –57.460*** [0.000]	Panel ADF-Statistic	–3.516*** [0.000]		
$Equation\,1B: MC_{it} = \beta_0 + \beta_1 CoalP_{it} + \beta_2 FuOlP_{it} + \beta_3 GasP_{it} + \beta_4 LerI_{Regit} + \varepsilon_{it}$	G_T –5.505*** [0.000]	Panel v-Statistic	1.629* [0.063]	Group rho-Statistic	–131.619*** [0.000]
	G_α –106.822*** [0.000]	Panel rho-Statistic	–143.220*** [0.000]	Group PP-Statistic	–49.662***[0.000]
	P_T –13.852*** [0.000]	Panel PP-Statistic	–50.268*** [0.000]	Group ADF-Statistic	–4.165*** [0.000]
	P_α –108.782*** [0.000]	Panel ADF-Statistic	–4.102*** [0.000]		
$Equation\,2A: SQ_{it} = \beta_0 + \beta_1 PurchQ_{it} + \beta_2 MC_{it} + \beta_3 LerI_{noRegit} + \varepsilon_{it}$	G_T –4.757*** [0.000]	Panel v-Statistic	2.716*** [0.003]	Group rho-Statistic	–51.502*** [0.000]
	G_α –60.334*** [0.000]	Panel rho-Statistic	–52.455*** [0.000]	Group PP-Statistic	–24.878*** [0.000]
	P_T –11.548*** [0.000]	Panel PP-Statistic	–24.810*** [0.000]	Group ADF-Statistic	–4.707*** [0.000]
	P_α –54.626** *[0.000]	Panel ADF-Statistic	–4.644*** [0.000]		
$Equation\,2B: SQ_{it} = \beta_0 + \beta_1 PurchQ_{it} + \beta_2 MC_{it} + \beta_3 LerI_{Regit} + \varepsilon_{it}$	G_T –4.682*** [0.000]	Panel v-Statistic	2.322*** [0.010]	Group rho-Statistic	–52.006*** [0.000]
	G_α –59.936*** [0.000]	Panel rho-Statistic	–52.763*** [0.000]	Group PP-Statistic	–25.178*** [0.000]
	P_T –11.134*** [0.000]	Panel PP-Statistic	–24.914*** [0.000]	Group ADF-Statistic	–4.764*** [0.000]
	P_α –49.431*** [0.000]	Panel ADF-Statistic	–4.579*** [0.000]		
$Equation\,3A: NetQ_{it} = \beta_0 + \beta_1 MC_{it} + \beta_2 LerI_{noRegit} + \varepsilon_{it}$	G_T –5.460*** [0.000]	Panel v-Statistic	1.568* [0.058]	Group rho-Statistic	–38.280*** [0.000]
	G_α –73.812*** [0.000]	Panel rho-Statistic	–30.588*** [0.000]	Group PP-Statistic	–19.848*** [0.000]
	P_T –12.963***	Panel PP-Statistic	–16.283***	Group	–4.436***

	[0.000]		[0.000]	ADF-Statistic	[0.000]
	P_α −62.119***	Panel	−3.679***		
	[0.000]	ADF-Statistic	[0.000]		
$Equation\,3B: NetQ_{it} = \beta_0 + \beta_1 MC_{it} + \beta_2 LerI_{Regit} + \varepsilon_{it}$	G_T −5.341***	Panel v-Statistic	0.7152*	Group	−33.239***
	[0.000]		[0.237]	rho-Statistic	[0.000]
	G_α −72.295***	Panel rho-Statistic	−21.420***	Group	−16.654***
	[0.000]		[0.000]	PP-Statistic	[0.000]
	P_T −11.964***	Panel PP-Statistic	−12.786***	Group	−3.608***
	[0.000]		[0.000]	ADF-Statistic	[0.000]
	P_α −51.816***	Panel	−2.112**		
	[0.000]	ADF-Statistic	[0.017]		

Notes: Tests results were generated by Eviews and 'x twest' Stata module. Pedroni's Panel statistics as well as all of Westerlund's are weighted. Dep. var. of coint. reg. = dependent variable of the cointegrating regression. Values in [] are robust p-values generated through bootstrapping because of cross-sectional dependence in the residuals. *, **, and *** indicate significance at 10%, 5%, and 1%, respectively.

Table 3. Panel cointegration tests results.

Overall, according to the results displayed in **Table 3** for the three equations, it is possible to claim that all variables (quantity purchased in wholesale market to sell in open market, coal price, fuel-oil price, gas price, marginal cost, net quantity, Lerner index 1, and Lerner index 2) are cointegrated, i.e., we have uncovered meaningful long-run relationships.

3.6. Estimation of the cointegration vector

The traditional specification of Autoregressive Distributed Lag [ARDL (p, q)] is normally used for the estimation of dynamic heterogeneous panels [45] through the following equation: $y_{it} = \sum_{j=1}^{p} \lambda_{it} \times y_{i,t-j} + \sum_{j=0}^{q} \delta_{ij}^{'} \times X_{i,t-j} + \mu_i + \varepsilon_{it}$, in which p is the number of lags of the dependent variable, q is the number of lags of the explanatory variables, $i = 1, 2, \ldots, N$, $t = 1, 2, \ldots, T$, X_{it} is a vector $(k-1)$ of explanatory variables, δ_{ij} is a vector of unknown parameters, λ_{it} are scalars and μ_{it} is a specific term associated to each company.

It is possible to infer what deviations from the long-term equilibrium of the variables influence the short-term dynamics after assuring both the nonstationarity of the variables of the equation and the presence of cointegration among them. The answer to these deviations can be represented by an ECM represented by the following equation: $\Delta y_{it} = \phi_i \left(y_{i,t-1} - \theta_i^{'} \times X_{it} \right) + \sum_{j=1}^{p-1} \lambda_{ij}^{*} \times \Delta y_{i,t-j} + \sum_{j=0}^{q-1} \delta_{ij}^{'*} \times \Delta X_{i,t-j} + \mu_i + \varepsilon_{it}$, in which $\phi_i = -\left(1 - \sum_{j=1}^{p} \lambda_{ij}\right)$, $\theta_i = \sum_{j=0}^{q} \delta_{ij} / \left(1 - \sum_k \lambda_{ik}\right)$, $\lambda_{ij}^{*} = -\sum_{m=j+1}^{p} \lambda_{im}$, with $j = 1, 2, \ldots, p-1$ and $\delta_{ij}^{'*} = -\sum_{m=j+1}^{q} \delta_{im}$, with $j = 1, 2, \ldots, q-1$.

The speed of adjustment from the error correction term, ϕ_i, and the vector of parameter of long-run equilibrium relationship, θ_i, will be given particular attention. It is expected that the former would be different from zero and would be significantly negative under the assumption that the variables return to their long-run equilibrium.

The equation is estimated according to the assumptions made regarding the homogeneity of the short- and long-term parameters among the panel of companies.

For the panel cointegration estimation, we will use several estimation methodologies: the Pooled Mean Group (PMG), the Full Modified Ordinary Least Squares (FMOLS), and the Dynamic Ordinary Least Squares (DOLS).

All intercepts, ratios, and variances of the errors vary between the groups [46]. Although the PMG method allows the error variances, the short-run coefficients and the intercepts differ freely across groups, but it restricts the long-run coefficients to be similar throughout the panel as the method assumes dynamic fixed-effects [46].

As electric power firms operating in the same market are submitted to the same regulatory policies and movements in international fossil fuels prices, the long-run equilibrium relationships between the variables are expected to be similar between groups. Accordingly, the PMG method may be of interest.

Due to the greater flexibility in the presence of heterogeneity in the cointegration vectors and to the lower size distortion vis-à-vis the estimators within groups, we will complement our analysis using FMOLS and DOLS methods, as recommended by Pedroni [47].

Table 4 reports the long- and short-run estimates, based on different estimation strategies adopted. The results of FMOLS and DOLS techniques, displayed in the first two columns, provide information on the long-run relationship between marginal cost and independent variables included in Eq. 1A (absence of regulation) and Eq. 1B (presence of regulation). For each variable, the panel estimates are remarkably similar in sign and magnitude across the two techniques.

For the panel results, the prices of coal price and fuel-oil are negative, in the absence of regulation, while the price of gas is positive, statistically significant, but not similar in value across the FMOLS and DOLS estimation techniques. For example, 1 unit increase in the prices of coal, fuel-oil, and gas raises marginal costs by –0.061 €/MWh, –0.056 €/MWh, and 0.086 €/MWh, respectively, using the FMOLS estimator or –0.034 €/MWh, –0.058 €/MWh, and 0.063 €/MWh, respectively, using the DOLS estimator.

On the other hand, in the presence of regulation, 1 unit increase in the prices of coal, fuel-oil, and gas raises marginal costs by 0.1579 €/MWh, –0.1088 €/MWh, and –0.0589 €/MWh, respectively, using the FMOLS estimation technique, or by 0.1649 €/MWh, –0.1065 €/MWh, and –0.0892 €/MWh, respectively, using the DOLS estimation technique.

The Lerner index 1 (absence of regulation) is negative and the Lerner index 2 (presence of regulation) is positive, both statistically significant on marginal costs per power plant, using FMOLS or DOLS techniques.

There is a statistically significant effect for all independent variables on marginal costs, both in the absence and in the presence of regulation, when using the PMG estimation. In the

http://dx.doi.org/10.5772/62953

presence of regulation, the speed of adjustment is negative, as expected, but its magnitude (0.26) is somewhat large when compared to the value in the absence of regulation. This implies that the PMG model, in the presence of regulation, does return immediately to its equilibrium after a shock pushes it away from the steady state. On the other hand, in the absence of regulation, the PMG model does not immediately return to its equilibrium after a shock, as the magnitude (0.086) is somewhat small. In fact, as the convergence coefficient (error correction term) is statistically significant, it provides further evidence of the existence of a long-run relationship between the marginal costs and the explanatory variables.

The results of the long-run and short-run relationships show that the PMG estimates of the Lerner index in the absence of regulation have a negative statistically significant impact on marginal cost (–7.527 €/MWh for the long-run and –22.446 €/MWh, for the short-run). In the presence of regulation, the estimates for the Lerner index show positive impacts in the long-run relationships (9.280 €/MWh) and negative impacts in the short-run (–2.383 €/MWh).

$Equation1A : MC_{it} = \beta_0 + \beta_1 CoalP_{it} + \beta_2 FuOlP_{it} + \beta_3 GasP_{it} + \beta_4 LerI_{noRegit} + \varepsilon_{it}$

	FMOLS	DOLS	PMG
Dependent variable:	Marginal Cost	Marginal Cost	Δ Marginal Cost
Convergent coefficients			–0.08632***
			(0.014)
Long-run coefficients			
Coal price	–0.06015***	–0.03454	–0.05616*
	(0.0202)	(0.0228)	(0.0312)
Fuel-oil price	–0.0564***	–0.0584***	–0.0387***
	(0.0060)	(0.0064)	(0.0096)
Gas price	0.0863**	0.06382	–0.1901***
	(0.0366)	(0.0404)	(0.061)
Lerner index 1	–8.8457***	–7.5481***	–7.5271***
	(0.708)	(0.943)	(1.1093)
Short-run coefficients			
Δ Coal price			0.01844***
			(0.0050)
Δ Fuel-oil price			–0.01135***
			(0.0027)
Δ Gas Price			0.08198***
			(0.0162)
Δ Lerner Index 1			–22.4461***
			(1.900)
Hausman test ($\varkappa^2$)			8.26(0.142)

	FMOLS	DOLS	PMG
R-square (r^2)	0.541	0.658	

$$Equation1B : MC_{it} = \beta_0 + \beta_1 CoalP_{it} + \beta_2 FuOlP_{it} + \beta_3 GasP_{it} + \beta_4 LerI_{Regit} + \varepsilon_{it}$$

	FMOLS	DOLS	PMG
Dependent variable:	Marginal Cost	Marginal Cost	Δ Marginal Cost
Convergent coefficients			–0.26326***
			(0.0463)
Long-run coefficients			
Coal price	0.1579***	0.16495***	0.16448***
	(0.017)	(0.0186)	(0.0179)
Fuel-oil Price	–0.1088***	–0.1065***	–0.09682***
	(0.005)	(0.0059)	(0.0057)
Gas price	–0.0589*	–008928**	–0.08123**
	(0.034)	(0.0395)	(0.0364)
Lerner Index 2	10.420***	10.6046***	9.2799***
	(0.460)	(0.542)	(0.4887)
Short-run coefficients			
Δ Coal price			–0.00912
			(0.0169)
Δ Fuel-oil Price			0.00749
			(0.0120)
Δ Gas Price			–0.04196
			(0.0315)
Δ Lerner Index 2			–2.3828***
			(0.5823)
Hausman test ($\varkappa^2$)			1.19
			(0.945)
R-square (r^2)	0.483	0.564	
No. of firms	6	6	6
No. of observations	9756	9756	9846

Notes: All equations include a constant sector-specific term. Values in () are standard errors. ***, ** and * indicate significance at the 1%, 5%, and 10% levels, respectively.

Table 4. panel cointegration estimation results.

Table 5 presents the results of the model specifying the quantity sold as the dependent variable, and **Table 6** presents the results of the model specifying the net quantity as the dependent variable, when the marginal cost and other explanatory variables are the independent variables. The focus in now on how the marginal costs, and the Lerner indexes affect bid quantities. The results suggest that the coefficients are consistently positive across the alternative estimators and also highly significant.

When analyzing the long-run effect, the coefficients in Eqs 2A and 2B of the quantity purchased in wholesale market to sell in open market reveal a statistical and significant effect on the quantity sold in wholesale market (0.851 MWh or 0.858 MWh, in the absence of regulation, and 0.893 MWh or 0.910 MWh, in the presence of regulation, respectively, using FMOLS or DOLS estimators).

The marginal cost, show a positive effect and statistically significant at the 1% level on the quantity sold in the wholesale market, in the absence and presence of regulation. The Lerner indexes, both in the absence and in the presence of regulation, are also positive and statistically significant, but the difference between FMOLS and DOLS estimates is large: in absence of regulation, this means, the increase of market power induces an increase in the quantity sold around 14,183 and 15,485 MWh, whereas in the presence of regulation the increase is between 8040 and 7388 MWh.

The results show that the PMG estimates of the marginal costs have, in the absence of regulation, a statistically significant positive impact on the sold quantity both in the long-run (1983.37 MWh) and in the short-run (584.46 MWh). In the presence of regulation, we also found a positive impact on marginal cost in long-run relationships (1578.91 MWh) as well as in the short-run relationships (468.98 MWh).

In the absence of regulation, we found that the Lerner index has a positive effect on the sold quantity, both in the long-run as well as in the short run.

Table 6 shows that the Lerner index and marginal costs provide statistically significant effects on net quantities using FMOLS or DOLS estimators, former being negative and the latter positive, both in the absence and in the presence of regulation.

In general, throughout all equations, although the DOLS method has generated coefficients with values slightly higher than those obtained by the FMOLS method, we can conclude that the long-run results obtained by both methods, DOLS and FMOLS, are suited to the analysis.

Equation2A : $SQ_{it} = \beta_0 + \beta_1 PurchQ_{it} + \beta_2 MC_{it} + \beta_3 LerI_{noRegit} + \varepsilon_{it}$

	FMOLS	DOLS	PMG
Dependent variable:	Sold quantity	Sold quantity	Δ Sold quantity
Convergent coefficients			–0.0524***(0.0136)
Long-run coefficients			
Purchased quantity to sell in open market	0.85117***(0.025)	0.8577***(0.0280)	0.98543***(0.0701)
Marginal costs	1429.80***(83.823)	1411.846***(101.703)	1983.37***(226.57)
Lerner Index 1	14182.94***(2559.34)	15484.80***(3198.87)	127935.86***(6646.40)
Short-run coefficients			

Δ Purchased quantity to sell in open market			0.26344***(0.082)
Δ Marginal costs			584.46***(195.95)
Δ Lerner Index 1			4066.38**1659.99)
Hausman test ($\varkappa^2$)			–3.91
R-square (r^2)	0.665	0.610	
$Equation2B: SQ_{it} = \beta_0 + \beta_1 PurchQ_{it} + \beta_2 MC_{it} + \beta_3 LerI_{Regit} + \varepsilon_{it}$			
	FMOLS	DOLS	PMG
Dependent variable:	Sold quantity	Sold quantity	Δ Sold quantity
Convergent coefficients			–0.04979***(0.0108)
Long-run coefficients			
Purchased quantity to sell in open market	0.89339***(0.023)	0.91021***(0.0260)	1.00889***(0.0708)
Marginal costs	1141.84***(80.538)	1151.06***(101.76)	1578.91***(229.45)
Lerner Index 2	8039.68***(1648.76)	7388.14***(190.72)	4001.013(4522.50)
Short-run coefficients			
Δ Purchased quantity to sell in open market			0.2312***(0.075)
Δ Marginal costs			468.98***(181.35)
Δ Lerner Index 2			8317.59**(3439.04)
Hausman test ($\varkappa^2$)			114.39***(0.000)
R-square (r^2)	0.777	0.728	
No. of firms	6	6	6
No. of observations	9756	9756	9846

Notes: All equations include a constant sector-specific term. Values in () are standard errors. ***, ** and * indicate significance at the 1%, 5%, and 10% levels, respectively.

Table 5. Panel cointegration estimation results.

$Equation3A: NetQ_{it} = \beta_0 + \beta_1 MC_{it} + \beta_2 LerI_{noRegit} + \varepsilon_{it}$			
	FMOLS	DOLS	PMG
Dependent variable:	Net quantity	Net quantity	Δ Net quantity
Convergent coefficients			–0.1627*(0.101)
Long-run coefficients			
Marginal costs	1454.20***(218.61)	1676.32***(258.24)	–2571.88*** (675.32)
Lerner Index 1	–28065.29*** (6882.92)	–29532.90*** (8402.43)	–25764.33 (17632.3)

http://dx.doi.org/10.5772/62953

Short-run coefficients			
Δ Marginal costs			685.706***(209.12)
Δ Lerner Index 1			15214.38***(4463.26)
Hausman test ($\varkappa^2$)			17.41(0.000)
R-square (r^2)	0.722	0.738	
$Equation3B : NetQ_{it} = \beta_0 + \beta_1 MC_{it} + \beta_2 LerI_{Regit} + \varepsilon_{it}$			
	FMOLS	DOLS	PMG
Dependent variable:	Net quantity	Net quantity	Δ Net quantity
Convergent coefficients			–0.06206***(0.0180)
Long-run coefficients			
Marginal costs	2043.93***(210.13)	2213.19***(259.70)	108.536(75.413)
Lerner Index 2	–21207.82***(4885.84)	–20263.54***(5707.98)	9537.00***(1467.26)
Short-run coefficients			
Δ Marginal costs			251.508*(141.10)
Δ Lerner Index 2			–8014.105(10323.91)
Hausman test ($\varkappa^2$)			4.89(0.179)
R-square (r^2)	0.724	0.740	
No. of firms	6	6	6
No. of observations	9756	9756	9846

Notes: All equations include a constant sector-specific term. Values in () are standard errors. ***, ** and * indicate significance at the 1%, 5% and 10% levels, respectively.

Table 6. panel cointegration estimation results.

4. Discussion and regulatory implications

All the results of the estimation of the relationship between marginal costs, the Lerner indexes, and bid quantities justify some reflections on the implications of regulatory policy in the period analyzed for this electricity market. Our results suggest that the coefficients are consistently positive across the alternative estimators and also highly significant. The marginal cost, show a positive effect and is statistically significant at the 1% level on the quantity sold in the wholesale market in the absence and the presence of regulation. The Lerner indexes, both in the absence and in the presence of regulation, are also positive and statistically significant.

With these evidences it is possible to claim that the exercise of market power is explained by the dominance the two major players have over the various technologies underlying the quantities that are bid in the market pool, which involve technologies with high fixed costs and low variable costs operating almost continuously over time (case of coal plants) so that their remuneration is determined by setting hourly rates of the day throughout the year, with closing prices above marginal production costs for these plants. With high variable cost technologies, whose production is discontinuous and dependent on exogenous variables such as hydraulicity and wind intensity, bids in periods of high demand may be justified given the capacity constraints of coal plants. For that reason, the market overcompensates some technologies and subcompensates others due to unpredictable phenomena at the moment of production shifts. This adjustment is not possible in the electricity generation sector because most investments are not replicable and because the existence of sunk costs discourage the abandonment of technologies whose compensation does not cover average costs, but only the variable costs, so the discrepancies persist. As such, the intervention of regulatory mechanisms is needed to create the necessary conditions for resizing the capacity. On the other hand, the prevalence of market power exercise reflects different vectors of efficiency (efficiency in resource allocation, technical efficiency, and production scale efficiency) of the various market players, especially between the two major firms, Endesa and Iberdrola, and other remaining companies operating in the spot electricity market. The inefficiency caused by the misallocation of resources has theoretically minimum consequences, but we need to know the elasticity of demand, the increase in prices caused by market power, and the slope of the average costs of companies exercising market power. The (allocative) market efficiency variation caused by one (or more) of the reasons abovementioned can nearly always be corrected by means of regulatory actions

Our results show that the presence of the CTC regulatory mechanism has a positive, artificial effect on marginal costs. During the period of analysis, the supply of the two largest companies in the electricity market is based on the coal (Endesa) and hydroelectric power (Iberdrola). The creation of this compensatory mechanism for the sunk costs of electricity producers basically smoothen out the fluctuations of the final price of electricity in the pool. In this way, it behaves as a maximum price. On the other hand, CTCs also constitute a control mechanism of capacity payments requiring a certain level of activity investment in the various technologies over time. Considering that in the period of analysis, the level of CTC has been set higher than the market equilibrium prices, which in turn are smaller than the marginal cost of those technologies, it is expected that the market power effect has a positive signal in what pertains to the marginal cost associated with technologies with lower variable costs.

The price cap criterion used by the Spanish authorities to mitigate the market power was very important in the transition context of the Spanish electricity market. The incentives provided by the regulation interfered with the day-ahead market and led to lower prices than the ones practiced by the profit maximization behavior. As we observed, during 2002–2006, there were significant differences between real prices and marginal costs and between real prices and the regulated price cap. As a consequence, they were taken into account when analyzing the marker power indexes in the absence and in the presence of regulation.

In other words, it is possible to contend that the CTCs served as an incentive bid for the purchase and sale of electricity at low prices. Moreover, they do not promote competition as predicted with the liberalization of the market because it discourages the entry of new market players and reinforce the dominant position of large power firms, likely leading to price wars and collusion as had been admitted by Fabra and Toro [15].

On the other hand, the scope of the CTCs, as a market power mitigation mechanism, appears to be virtual as well, since this same mitigation was achieved considering that the players altogether exercise net demander and net supplier behaviors, i.e., that majority of sales bids are lower than the majority of purchase bids in the OMEL market for sale in the open market, otherwise, there is a strengthening in the exercise of market power can occur. The net supplier (Endesa) and net demander (Iberdrola) assumptions behaviors are in line with what has been admitted and referenced by Kühn and Machado [4] and Ciarreta and Espinosa [2], and reinforces the idea of collusion admitted by Fabra and Toro [15].

Our results of this study are tuned with the previous studies [48] corroborating that in order to mitigate the market power problem in OMEL electricity spot market and to ensure the functioning of competitive market conditions, it would be necessary to strengthen regulatory intervention that seems to have been scarce and ineffective. As a result, it is suggested that in order to complement the regulatory compensatory incentive mechanism to sunk costs through implementation of CTCs, the establishment of the rate of return of setting rules for investment decisions should also have been implemented in order to ensure the desired remodeling of electricity generation as established by Directive 2001/77/EC of the European Parliament and by the Council on the promotion of electricity produced from renewable energy sources in the internal electricity market.

The idea of this type of regulation (Rate of return) is that revenues should cover the costs so that economic profit is controlled, and there are no financial transfers to the company. As such, it is expected that the regulated company will obtain an adequate return based on the investment carried out.

However, as has been accepted by Biglaiser and Riordan [49], under the regulation involving the price-cap, cost reduction is more likely to occur in the early years of a regulatory regime, since the setting of ceilings for the revenues of the players are set up based on an established cost review for a given period. As such, it seems questionable to use such procedures in the implementation of CTC mechanisms, since it was expected to expire in 2010 when it was terminated in 2006. This anticipated recovery of sunk costs was associated with larger differences between the market price and marginal costs generating higher mark-ups, and consequently higher profits for market players and greater market power. As such, the regulation was ineffective or nonexistent to ensure the desirable conditions of effective competition in the electricity market.

5. Conclusion

In the Spanish electricity market, the major relationship between production and commercialization is characterized by the (bilateral) contract between the producer and the distributor, in which this technical and commercial relationship is not subject to regulation. In order to answer the first posed question, under the promotion of competition assumption, where the market price should be equal to marginal cost, our results show that fuel prices exercise mixed impact effects on marginal costs per power plant (coal, oil, gas, CCGT, nuclear, and hydro-electric). The two measures of market power exercise proposed show statistically significant effects on marginal costs both in the long- and short-run. In the long-run, as a significant reduction on marginal costs in the absence of regulation and an increase in the marginal cost in the presence of regulation, as far as FMOLS or DOLS estimators are concerned. In the short-run, there is a decrease on marginal costs in the absence of regulation and a small decrease on marginal costs for the entire panel considered, according to the PMG estimator.

Related to the second posed question, our results point to the significant inclusion of net seller's behavior strategies in the Spanish electricity market, both in the absence and in the presence of regulation. In the long-term and short-term, the Lerner Indexes, marginal costs, and purchased quantity to sell in open market have a significantly positive impact on the sold quantity, under and in the absence of regulation, as far as the FMOLS, DOLS, and PMG estimators are concerned.

Answering to the last question, our results point to the significant inclusion of net quantity behavior strategies in the Spanish electricity market. In the long-term, the Lerner Indexes and marginal costs have a significantly negative and positive impact on the net quantity, respectively, under and in the absence of regulation, as far as the FMOLS and DOLS estimators are concerned.

These two statistically significant evidences found through the two abovementioned models allow, on the one hand, admitting that the scope of promoting the CTC regulatory mechanism to compensate for the sunk costs of power companies operating in OMEL market was successfully achieved and faster than expected based on the performance of the largest electricity producers. These strategic bidding behavior and capacity withholding involve generating firms bidding some prices above the variable production costs of their units with the intent of forcing the market-clearing price above competitive levels.

Based on this evidence, and as referred to in the previous section, the great novelty of this work demands a closer look at virtually nonexistent regulatory policies during an important period of transition to competition in the Spanish electricity market, and under a strong market power exercise by two major players. As such, we think that during the period under analysis, the market operator should have given the electricity market regulating entity room for intervention in the market with the implementation of the rate-of-return mechanism. This type of regulation would have as major constraint that revenues should cover costs so that the economic profit could be controlled, and there are no financial transfers to the electricity company. In this way, it is expected to obtain an adequate return based on the size of the investment carried out by the company, either with the transition to competition or with the introduction of new production plants with cleaner technologies.

http://dx.doi.org/10.5772/62953

Author details

Victor M. F. Moutinho, António C. Moreira* and Jorge H. Mota

*Address all correspondence to: amoreira@ua.pt

Department of Economics, Management, Industrial Engineering, and Tourism, University of Aveiro, Portugal

References

[1] Ciarreta, A., Espinosa, M. P. Supply function competition in the Spanish wholesale electricity market. Energy Journal. 2010; 31(4): 137–158.

[2] Ciarreta, A., Espinosa, M. The impact of regulation on pricing behavior in the Spanish electricity market (2002–2005). Energy Economics. 2012;34(6): 2039–2045.

[3] Ciarreta, A., Espinosa, M. P. Market power in the Spanish electricity auction. Journal of Regulatory Economics. 2010; 37(1): 42–69.

[4] Kühn, K., Machado, M. Bilateral market power and vertical integration in the Spanish electricity spot market. CEPR Discussion Papers, Madrid. 2004; 4590.

[5] Neuhoff, K., Barquin, J., Boots, M., Ehrenmann, A., Hobbs, B., Rijkers, F. Network constrained Cournot models of liberalized electricity markets: The devil is in the details. Energy Economics. 2005; 27(3):495–525.

[6] Baldick, R., Grant, R., Kahn, E. Theory and application of linear supply function equilibrium in electricity markets. Journal of Regulatory Economics. 2004; 252:143–167.

[7] Holmberg, P. Asymmetric supply function equilibrium with constant marginal costs. Energy Journal. 2007; 28(2):55–82.

[8] Fabra, N., von der Fehr, N., Harbord, D. Modeling electricity auctions. The Electricity Journal. 2002; 15(7):72–81.

[9] Joskow, P., Kahn, E. A quantitative analysis of pricing behavior in California's wholesale electricity market during Summer 2000. Energy Journal. 2002; 0(4):1–35.

[10] Borenstein, S., Bushnell, J., Wolak, F. Measuring market inefficiencies in California's restructured wholesale electricity market. The American Economic Review. 2002; 92(5): 1376–1405.

[11] Wolak, F.A. Measuring unilateral market power in wholesale electricity markets: The California market, 1998–2000. American Economic Review. 2003; 93(2):425–430.

[12] Furió, D., Lucia, J.J.. Congestion management rules and trading strategies in the Spanish electricity market. Energy Economics. 2009; 31(1):48–60.

[13] Moutinho, V., Moreira, A. C, Mota, J. Evaluating the strategic supply per power plant: evidence from the Spanish wholesale electricity market. International Journal of Energy Technology and Policy. 2015; 11(2):97–126.

[14] Moutinho, V., Moreira, A. C., Mota, J. Measuring the simultaneous quantity game in the OMEL spot electricity market. International Journal of Energy Economics and Policy. 2015; 5(1):305–320.

[15] Fabra, N., Toro, J. Price wars and collusion in the Spanish electricity market. International Journal of Industrial Organization. 2005; 23(3/4):155–181.

[16] Moutinho, V., Vieira, J., Moreira, A. C. The crucial relationship among energy commodity prices: Evidence from the Spanish electricity market. Energy Policy. 2011; 39(10):5898–5908.

[17] García-Martín, J. A. Spot market competition with stranded costs in the Spanish electricity industry. WP 0106. 2001;CEMFI, Madrid.

[18] Linares, P., Labandeira, X. Energy efficiency: Economics and policy. Journal of Economic Surveys. 2004; 24(3):573–592.

[19] Linares, P., Santos, F., Pérez-Arriaga, I. Scenarios for the evolution of the Spanish electricity sector: is it on the right path towards sustainability? Energy Policy. 2008; 36(11):4057–4068.

[20] Grobman, J., Carey, J. Price caps and investment: long-run effects in the electric generation industry. Energy Policy. 2001; 29(7):545–552.

[21] Stoft, S. Power System Economics: Designing Markets for Electricity. Piscataway, NJ: Wiley-Interscience; 2002.

[22] Joskow, P., Tirole, J. Reliability and competitive electricity markets. The RAND Journal of Economics. 2007; 38(1):60–84.

[23] Biglaiser, G., Riordan, M. Dynamics of price regulation. The RAND Journal of Economics. 2000; 31:744–767.

[24] Baldursson, F. Irreversible investment under uncertainty in oligopoly. Journal of Economic Dynamics and Control. 1998; 22(4):627–644.

[25] Lambrecht, B. The impact of debt financing on entry and exit in a duopoly. The Review of Financial Studies. 2001; 14(3):765–804.

[26] Grenadier, S. Option exercise games: An application to the equilibrium investment strategies of firms. The Review of Financial Studies. 2002; 15(3):691–721.

[27] Earle, R., Schmedders, K., Tatur, T. On price caps under uncertainty. The Review of Economic Studies. 2007; 74(1):93–111.

[28] Levin, A, Lin C-F., Chu C-S., J. Unit root tests in panel data: asymptotic and finite-sample properties. Journal of Econometrics. 2002; 108(1):1–24.

[29] Breitung, J. The local power of some unit root tests for panel data. In: Baltagi, B. H., Fomby, T., Hill, R (Eds), Nonstationary panels, panel cointegration, and dynamic panels. Advances in Econometrics, Vol. 15. London: Emerald Group Publishing Limited; 2001. pp. 161–177.

[30] Hadri, K. Testing for stationarity in heterogeneous panel data. The Econometrics Journal. 2000; 3(2):148–161.

[31] Im, K., Pesaran, M., Shin, Y. Testing for unit roots in heterogeneous panels. Journal of Econometrics. 2003; 115(1):53–74.

[32] Lagarto, J., Sousa, J., Martins, Á. The impact of the Iberian electricity market on the competitive behavior of generating companies using a conjectural variations approach. In: 7th International Conference on the European Energy Market (EEM); 23–25th June; Madrid. 2010.

[33] Holmberg, P., Newbery, D. The supply function equilibrium and its policy implications for wholesale electricity auctions. Utilities Policy. 2010; 18(4):209–226.

[34] Vives, X. Strategic supply function competition with private information. Econometrica. 2011; 79(6):1919–1966.

[35] Ciarreta, A. A note on strategic delegation: The role of decreasing returns to scale. Economics Bulletin. 2009; 29(1):277–285.

[36] Choi, I. Unit root tests for panel data. Journal of International Money and Finance. 2001; 20(2):249–272.

[37] Maddala, G., Wu, S. A comparative study of unit root tests with panel data and a new simple test. Oxford Bulletin of Economics and Statistics. 1999; 61(S1):631–652.

[38] Pesaran, H. A simple panel unit root test in the presence of cross-section dependence. Journal of Applied Econometrics. 2007; 22(2):265–312.

[39] Mahadevan, R., Asafu-Adjaye, J. Energy consumption, economic growth and prices: A reassessment using panel VECM for developed and developing countries. Energy Policy. 2007; 35(4):2481-2490.

[40] Engle, R., Granger, C. Co-integration and error-correction: Representation, estimation and testing. Econometrica. 1987;55(2):251–276.

[41] Pedroni, P. Critical values for cointegration tests in heterogeneous panels with multiple regressors. Oxford Bulletin of Economics and Statistics. 1999; 61(S1):653–678.

[42] Pedroni, P. Panel cointegration; asymptotic and finite sample properties of pooled time series tests with an application to the PPP hypothesis. Econometric Theory. 2004;20(3): 597–625.

[43] Persyn, D., Westerlund, J. Error-correction-based cointegration tests for panel data. Stata Journal. 2008; 8(2):232–241.

[44] Westerlund, J. Testing for error correction in panel data. Oxford Bulletin of Economics and Statistics. 2007; 69(6):709–748.

[45] Blackburne III, E., Frank, M. Estimation of nonstationary heterogeneous panels. Stata Journal. 2007; 7(2):197–208.

[46] Pesaran, H., Shin, Y., and Smith, R. Pooled mean group estimation of dynamic heterogeneous panels. Journal of the American Statistical Association. 1999; 94(446):621–634.

[47] Pedroni, P. Purchasing power parity tests in cointegrated panels. Review of Economics and Statistics. 2001;83(4):727–731.

[48] Moutinho, V., Moreira, A. C., Mota, J. Do regulatory mechanisms promote competition and mitigate market power? Evidence from Spanish electricity market . Energy Policy. 2014; 68:403–412.

[49] Biglaiser, G., Riordan, M. Dynamics of price regulation . Rand Journal of Economics. 2000; 31(4):744–767.